D0306011

DISHONEST TO GOD

DISHONEST TO GOD

MARY WARNOCK

continuum

Published by the Continuum International Publishing Group

The Tower Building 80 Maiden Lane
11 York Road   Suite 704
London   New York
SE1 7NX   NY 10038

www.continuumbooks.com

Copyright © Mary Warnock, 2010

All rights reserved. No part of this publication may be reproduced or transmitted in any form or by any means, electronic or mechanical, including photocopying, recording or any information storage or retrieval system, without prior permission from the publishers.

First published 2010

British Library Cataloguing-in-Publication Data
A catalogue record for this book is available from the British Library.

ISBN 978-1441-12712-9

Designed and typeset by Tony Lansbury, Tonbridge, Kent.
Printed and bound in Great Britain by the MPG Books Group

Contents

Introduction

The idea of God (or of gods) is central to religion, and without it religion would not exist. A religious person should be able, without either embarrassment or irony, to make mention of the God in whom he or she believes. My concern in the following pages is to consider some aspects of the role of religion, and therefore the idea of God, in the twenty-first century, as it relates to legislation and politics. To discuss religion and politics historically would be a bold task, and one that only a professional historian could undertake. My aim is more modest. It is concerned with religion and politics as they are currently practised. It is the Christian religion and recent politics that is at the centre of my enquiry, though sometimes other religions may be relevant. It is impossible to exaggerate the influence of Christianity on our culture and traditions, but also on our political thought and legislative practice. However, important though the part played by Christianity has been, no one doubts that the Christian religion has now lost its dominant and taken-for-granted position in the lives of the majority of citizens, many of whom are totally ignorant of the text of the Bible and of what goes on in church, and for whom the word 'God' is meaningless except as an exclamation. It is necessary therefore to consider what part Christianity should continue to play in legislation and politics, and what influence it has and should have in Parliament, whose responsibility is to legislate for Christian and non-Christian alike.

In the Judaeo-Christian tradition, of which the Church of England is part, God has a triple role. First, He is the creator of the universe, and, as the climax of his creation, of human beings, formed in his own image. Then, second, for those human beings, he is the ultimate source of morality, having revealed his laws to them alone. Third, he is the object of reverence and love, and the source of hope. However flawed the world may be, however much suffering it contains, God has promised that somehow or other all will be well, for those who put their trust in him. For Christians, this promise was historically confirmed through the life and death of Jesus, sent to earth as both God and man, to show that God cares about individuals, and can grant them salvation at last, if they follow his commandments, newly revealed through the Messiah. For Christians, this God is tripartite, Father, Son and Holy Ghost. The third member of the Holy Trinity, the Holy Spirit, is the giver of hope, security and truth: '*Non vos relinquam orphanos*' ('I will not leave you comfortless'). Though death is, in one sense, the end, and though what happens after death is a mystery, yet somehow the sharpness of death is overcome by God, as is proved by the death and resurrection of Christ.

This is the tradition in which I was brought up, the tradition of the Church of England, and this is what forms the background of the culture within which I, and many others of my generation, feel at home. Indeed, as far as I myself am concerned, the Church of England has played a significant part in my life. I went to a High Church school; until I was in my mid-sixties, I never lived anywhere except in a cathedral city. Church music has been one of my greatest passions, and in Oxford, where I spent most of my adult life, there were almost unlimited opportunities to enjoy liturgy and sacred music.

At the present time, having for long been a minority interest, the question of religion, its truth or falsity, its relevance or irrelevance to the way we should think and should live our lives, has come back into prominence as a subject of debate and disagreement; not as fierce, perhaps, as the controversies in the latter part of the nineteenth century, but significant nevertheless, especially in the field of morals and politics. Avowed atheists, such as the ubiquitous Richard Dawkins, once a quite rare bearded and sandal-wearing breed, are now everywhere to be heard, and are matched by people asserting that, whatever the atheists may think of religion, God exists, the Bible is true and religion is on the increase all over the world. Statistically this seems to be a fact, for good or ill.

I personally would not at all want religion to come to an end, and I give some reasons for this in Chapter 5, below. But there were those at the end of the nineteenth century who predicted that it would necessarily decline and die, succumbing at last to science. Dawkins and other atheists assert that this time has come: that religion should now curl up and die, being not just untrue, but damagingly so. For my part, I have increasingly come to think that one ought to try to be a bit more clear-headed about what religion essentially is, and what, if any, authority it should command, and over whom. I have been much influenced in this both by the writings of the former Bishop of Edinburgh, Richard Holloway (see especially, *Godless Morality*, Canongate 1999, and *Doubts and Loves*, Canongate 2001) and by my former tutor and friend, Dennis Nineham, who, more than thirty years ago, wrote:

'The characteristic religious difficulty today is a metaphysical difficulty at least in this sense: where men seem to need help above all is at the level of the *imagination*. They need some way of envisaging such realities as God, creation and providence imaginatively in a way which does no violence to the rest of what they know to be true. They need to be able to mesh-in their religious symbols with the rest of their sensibility in the sort of way supranaturalist and messianic imagery meshed-in with the sensibility of 1st-century people.' [Emphasis added]

The problem is thus partly historical. We can, helped by long tradition and by a familiar culture, partly put ourselves in the place of the first disciples, the Gospel-writers. We can even partly understand St Paul, the true inventor of Christianity as a religion separate from Judaism. But their natural imagery is not ours, much as we may love it, and all its associations. This is because of all that we know that they did not. Our viewpoint is inevitably different, and we cannot honestly overlook the gap that exists between us and them, or pretend that it does not exist. It is the issue of this gap that I try to address in the following chapters, not as a theologian, but as someone above all interested in morality, politics and the law, as well as in the concept of imagination itself, which, as Dennis Nineham understood, is central to the very existence of religion. It hardly needs to be said that other animals are not religious, nor are they, like us, politicians or law-makers. Neither do they have the need to explain the world to themselves. It is the human imagination that both demands and supplies such all-embracing explanations; human beings alone need to place themselves in the universe as a whole, and religious belief has historically been their way of doing this. So I want, albeit within a very narrow and recent framework, to look at the ways in which religion should and should not influence our moral and political decision-making.

It is misleading to say that this country is already an entirely secular society; but it would be equally wrong to overlook the ambiguous position of religion within it, and the curious role that religion plays in political debates, different certainly from its role in the USA, but equally demanding of examination and equally prone to accusations of hypocrisy or downright dishonesty. Part of the difficulty of conducting any study such as this is that the British do not, on the whole, care to talk about religion, at least not about their personal beliefs. In a general way, as I have suggested, religion versus atheism has become a topic of public debate. But the debate is conducted in relatively abstract, or at least historical, terms, and does not involve too much in the way of private sentiments or aspirations. This has meant that it is often difficult to separate arguments according to whether they are religious or secular, and if I have misrepresented anyone's beliefs I can only apologise.

CHAPTER ONE

Life, Death and Authority:
A Legislative History – Part One

In 2003, in a Ditchley Foundation Lecture, Lord Bingham of Cornhill, formerly Lord Chief Justice, reflected on the changing tasks of judges at the beginning of the twenty-first century. One change that he noticed was the extent to which judges were being called upon to make overtly moral pronouncements in court. It is seldom possible now to assert that 'this is not a court of morals'. Many judgments, especially in the higher courts, turn on whether or not a human right has been violated; and this, in the absence of a Bill of Rights, or a body of precedent, is itself a moral judgement.

For instance, the question whether a human right has been violated in ordering the sterilisation of a mentally disabled adult is plainly a question of whether there are any circumstances in which it can be morally justifiable to carry out such an act. One could argue on Utilitarian[1] or consequentialist grounds that

---

1. When I use the word 'Utilitarian' I am referring to the philosophical and political theory whose author was Jeremy Bentham, and whose less unambiguously committed follower was John Stuart Mill. This is the theory that a good measure is one whose consequences lead to the greatest happiness of the greatest number. The word (without a capital letter) is often, confusingly, used in a derogatory sense, to describe a measure, or an argument that looks to purely materialistic or monetary advantages. I do not use it in this sense.

more good than harm would come out of the procedure, or at any rate that much harm would be avoided; on the other hand, according to the Roman Catholic theory of the inviolability of the human person, one could argue that it would always be wrong. It would also be wrong on the widely accepted medico-ethical grounds that informed consent is necessary before any such intervention may be carried out, and someone who is mentally disabled is incompetent, that is, unable to give consent. Whatever a court decided, probably on largely pragmatic grounds, in such a case, it would be at least the beginning of a precedent, and would doubtless be usefully referred to in later cases. But there is no pre-existing definitive list of human rights to which judges may turn to settle such questions. The United Nations Universal Declaration of Human Rights (1948) was more aspirational than binding in international law. It was an essentially moral pronouncement of how people ought, and especially ought not, to be treated.

To take another example: some years ago, an NHS hospital in Cambridgeshire refused to operate for a third time on a baby with a severe heart condition who had twice failed to respond to surgery. The popular press claimed that this was a denial of the baby's fundamental 'right to life'. The hospital argued not only that the baby had suffered enough, and the chances of her surviving a third operation were very small, but, bravely, that to operate in these circumstances would be a wrong use of scarce resources, and other babies who could benefit would be deprived of a cot in intensive care. If the parents had sued the hospital, the court would have been faced with an essentially moral question. Yet such questions are not just matters for individual conscience. Since the court has to decide them and since whatever becomes law, or an accepted interpretation of law, applies equally to everyone, they are also questions of public policy. It seems the distinction between public and private morality has become harder and harder to draw. A judge will, of course, be guided by his own sense of what is right in the particular case before him; but he must also consider how his judgment will affect general policy in the future.

As with judges, so with legislators. There seems to be an increasing number of situations in which legislation is required to regulate a practice which may intuitively seem to many people wrong, or which should be practised only if hedged about by conditions and safeguards for fear of abuse. In proposing and debating such legislation, members of Parliament must express and defend often sharply conflicting moral views. An example of such legislation was the 1956 Cruelty to Animals Act, and the subsequent updating in 2004 of the Animals (Scientific Procedures) Act regulating the use of animals in laboratories. No one was, needless to say, in favour of deliberate cruelty to animals; and most people held that what was needed in the new Act was some regulation of how animals should be treated in the course of research. But some thought that human beings had no moral entitlement to use other animals for their own purposes at all, whether in laboratories or in the farmyard (the view of Animal Rights campaigners, not I think represented by anyone in Parliament, but a forceful and dangerous group in the outside world); many held that, in general, such use was and had traditionally been justified, as the beneficent practice of dairy and pig farming, to say nothing of horse-racing, showed; and many held that in the case of the use of animals in research, the benefits to human health and welfare far outweighed the harm to the animals concerned. Strict regulation of animal use was the compromise, and, for this, legislation was an absolute requirement. Such legislation is always firmly founded on moral arguments.

Perhaps the most famous instance of such morally founded legislation since the Second World War was the legislation that abolished capital punishment in the UK in 1965. Some people supported this legislation on the general moral grounds that deliberately to kill anyone, even a convicted murderer, was wrong, others argued that the death penalty was morally dangerous, because if subsequent evidence appeared that showed there had been a wrongful conviction, it was by then too late to remedy it. Both arguments were overtly moralistic.

The other piece of legislation of the same period was that which decriminalised homosexual acts in private between consenting males. This was the outcome of the Wolfenden Report published in 1959, and the subject of a fierce theoretical and academic debate between Lord Justice Devlin and H. L. A. Hart, Professor of Jurisprudence in the University of Oxford at that time (see the lecture delivered in 1959 by Lord Devlin as the second Maccabaean Lecture in Jurisprudence of the British Academy, entitled 'Morality and the Criminal Law', and later published as part of *The Enforcement of Morals*, 1965 [1968]; and H. L. A. Hart, *Law, Liberty and Morality*, 1963, and *Essays in Jurisprudence and Philosophy*, 1983, Essay 11 – all published by Oxford University Press). In this dispute the issue was precisely the relation of the law to morality.

Fortunately, in both of these instances, parliament voted for a change in the law in the direction of liberality, giving a strong moral lead to the country as a whole, in the face of fierce opposition from some sections of the press and many individual diehards. The issues have not remained on the agenda, but they serve as an example of how law-making is governed by moral reasoning, and how what may be called public morality, expressed in the will of Parliament, can sometimes prevail over private convictions or the campaigns of the popular press.

The same cannot be said for those questions of law and morality that are the subject of this chapter and the next. I shall examine them in some detail since they are recent and unresolved, at least in the sense that they are sure to come back to Parliament again and again. All of them are questions involving life and death. The fundamental issue is whether there are circumstances in which it is morally justifiable deliberately to take the life of a human being, and whether, therefore, the law should permit this to occur in specified cases. It is plain that strong moral convictions are brought to the consideration of such issues, as they were to the two major pieces of legislation in the 1960s. And, as was true then, the moral principles invoked were often in conflict. My specific interest, in what follows, is whether those moral convictions that are derived from religious belief carry special authority. This will turn out to be a difficult question to answer, because of the historically intimate connection between religion and morality, and therefore the conceptual difficulty in separating the two domains. Those who hold strong religious views will of course suggest that there is not a mere difficulty in such an attempt, but an impossibility; and that such a separation should not be contemplated, not for logical but for moral reasons. However, as I hope to make clear, I believe that a separation is of great importance. It is probably an over-simplification to describe ours as now a secular society. But there is enough truth in the description to make it inappropriate and conceptually confusing to let morality and the law remain grounded and justified only in the name of religion.

The first issue I shall consider is that of abortion. In November 1965, Lord Silkin introduced a Private Member's Abortion Bill in the House of Lords, which received strong support at Second Reading and had an unopposed Third Reading in March 1966. However, Parliament was dissolved soon after that, and the Bill did not reach the statute book. At the time, the law covering abortion was contained in section 58 of the Offences Against the Person Act (1861). According to this section, to carry out an abortion was a criminal offence punishable by life imprisonment. However, the law had become uncertain. For one thing, no woman who had carried out an abortion on her own foetus had been charged for many years. More significantly, within the previous two years three different judges, when charges were brought against a doctor, had so interpreted the law as to make it lawful for a doctor to carry out an abortion when he had done so after concluding that the health of the woman would be seriously damaged if the pregnancy were to continue, and had so instructed the jury. The process in effect involved two doctors, the woman's GP and a gynaecologist or obstetrician, who had to be persuaded by the GP to proceed with the abortion. By the early 1960s many abortions were thus lawfully carried out, but it was not necessarily straightforward either for the woman or for her GP. The pregnant woman had to persuade her doctor that she was incapable of continuing the pregnancy without physical or mental harm; he, in turn, had to persuade a specialist of the same alleged facts. There were inevitable delays and uncertainty. Doctors were, for the most part, prepared to go along with this, in spite of the uncertainty involved, but many of them charged high fees for doing so. One of the aims of Lord Silkin's Bill was to remove this uncertainty, and also the social injustice involved in having to pay a fee for an abortion that only the relatively wealthy could afford. Exploitation by unscrupulous doctors was a real threat.

Lord Silkin also aimed to extend the scope of legal abortion beyond cases where the mother's health was supposed to be at risk; and, above all, to reduce the number of illegal, back-street abortions, which in 1965 were estimated at more than 100,000 a year, and on the increase. In 1964 there were 50 deaths from illegal abortions and approximately 40,000 cases of women admitted to hospital as the result of such abortions; yet fewer than 50 people were convicted of carrying them out.

Lord Silkin started another Bill in 1966, soon after the new parliament began, but in the event handed it over to the young Liberal MP, David Steel (now the Liberal Democrat peer, Lord

Steel) who had won the ballot for a private member's Bill in the House of Commons. This Bill had its Second Reading on 22 July 1966. Although by now opinion polls showed that a huge majority of the general public wanted the law changed, the Bill had a rough and slow passage through the House of Commons, which involved more than 104 hours of debate and at least one all-night sitting. It was much amended, and was considerably less liberal than the original Silkin Bill had been, by the time it came to the House of Lords. In its compromise form it finally became law late in 1967.

In its Second Reading, where principles rather than details were discussed, opposition to the Bill in both Houses came largely from those who, while favouring reform of the then-current legal position with its uncertainty and likely injustice, nevertheless objected to the clauses of the Bill that would widen its scope, to permit abortion for so-called social reasons. These were reasons concerned not with the immediate health of the mother, but with the general well-being of the family, including existing children; and in addition there was to be permitted abortion based on the desire of the mother not to give birth to a child who would be severely disabled. The objectors in both Houses wanted a highly restricted Bill, which would establish in statute the lawfulness of a doctor's carrying out an abortion if and only if continuing the pregnancy would be harmful to the life or the health of the mother. These people were specifically opposed to any widening of the scope of permissible abortion, but agreed nevertheless that the current law was too indeterminate.

There were others, however, who, though they reluctantly agreed that in the case of risk to the mother's life (not to her health) an abortion must be permitted, were completely opposed to any change in the law, on the grounds that this would breach the principle of the sanctity of human life. After all, they argued, a foetus is both human and alive and its life must therefore be

13

protected as much as that of any other human being (with the exception, in rare cases, of its mother).

Looking back at these debates, one remarkable thing is the extent to which the question of abortion was seen as a medical matter, the decision whether or not an abortion should be carried out a wholly medical decision. This partly explains the opposition to the 'social' clauses of the Bill. For example, speaking in the House of Lords Second Reading debate, the eminent surgeon, Lord Brock, objected to the social reasons for abortion, saying that if these clauses in the Bill remained, the 'boundaries of medical indications would have been overstepped'. And he claimed to be speaking for most of those obstetric surgeons who would actually carry out abortions. At least one speaker suggested that the dislike that doctors and nurses felt for abortion itself constituted a proof that it was wrong. Although several objectors expressed their fears that the Bill if it proceeded unamended would lead in the direction of Abortion on Demand, hardly anyone spoke of any right that a woman might have to decide for herself whether she wanted the pregnancy to continue (though it is true that the Abortion Law Reform Association, run by women, was quoted as holding that every woman has a right to choose an abortion, and every child a right to be born wanted. But this was quoted in the parliamentary debate, only to be derided). And although supporters of the Bill spoke of the distress and mental anguish of some women who sought an abortion, most spoke as if this were nothing other than a possible symptom to be weighed up by doctors as an indication, or not, for intervention. Neither feminism nor human rights had quite emerged as providing moral arguments, at least in the UK. Paternalism reigned, and it was the doctor who was the father, the woman the child, in the doctor/patient relationship.

There were some notable exceptions. In her winding-up speech in the House of Commons Second Reading debate, Renee Short spoke in favour of the Bill and against the amendment proposed by William Wells, MP for Walsall North, which would have denied the Bill a Second Reading and thus killed it. Her arguments were largely based on the numbers of women who favoured a change in the law, and on the sufferings of those who now sought an abortion. Again, Dr John Dunwoody (member for Falmouth and Camborne) addressed the objection that a change in the law would undermine respect for the sanctity of human life. He said: 'There is, I hope, more to life than merely survival and we should be also thinking about the quality of that survival.' He went on to paint a picture of a mother with a large number of children and burdened by poverty who could not face another pregnancy. 'If one looks at it in that light one can see that, far from undermining respect for the sanctity of human life, this Bill could enhance respect for human life in the fullest sense of the phrase.'

It is upon the principle of the sanctity of life that the Roman Catholic Church relies in its total opposition to abortion. It does not mean, of course, sanctity of life in 'the fullest sense' invoked by Dr Dunwoody. When Roman Catholics (and indeed the many others who use the phrase) speak of the sanctity of human life, they are speaking of the value not of any particular kind of life, but of human life itself, at whatever stage of development, whether conscious or unconscious, whether lasting indefinitely or lasting half an hour, whether enjoyable or wracked with pain and suffering. It is as if life is a kind of sacred fluid, in itself of intrinsic value, and to be found flowing in all human beings like blood. It is the psyche (to be translated either as life or as soul) that the Greeks believed inhabited every creature.

Aristotle was the first Greek philosopher or scientist to explore this concept in depth. He believed that the psyche entered the human embryo in various different forms at different times, first as the vegetable life, shared by all living things, then in addition, or replacing it, as the sensory life shared by all animals, including human animals, and finally as the rational life, common to all human beings, and unique to them. The question of when the destruction of an embryo or foetus becomes the destruction of a human life thus turns on when the fully human psyche, life or soul, enters the body. Aristotle's theory of the development of life after conception, set out in *Of the Generation of Animals*, was a kind of speculative biology, within his general metaphysical framework of different kinds of cause. His notion of conception was very different from ours. He had no idea of the existence of the ovum, but thought that conception was the congealing of the menstrual blood somehow brought about by the semen. The biological sciences advanced very little after Aristotle for the next thousand or more years, and so his whole theory was taken over almost unchanged by Thomas Aquinas, who died in 1274. It became the theory of ensoulment.

However, the soul had taken on a new significance since the birth of Christianity. Although the rational soul is referred to by Aristotle as 'divine', and although it apparently entered the human foetus mysteriously from outside, it was nevertheless a biological concept. There is no possibility of a rational soul existing except in a material animal body fit in size and constitution to receive it. For Christianity, however (and here it owes much more to Plato than to Aristotle), the soul has a sanctity of its own, being destined for immortality.

At any rate, Aquinas, following Aristotle, held that the human soul did not enter the body until forty days after conception in the case of males, ninety days in the case of females. The unique exception to this law was that of the birth of Jesus, whose human life, being the life of the Holy Spirit, had come into being at the moment of conception, without going through the vegetable and animal developmental phases. Like Aristotle, Aquinas did not believe that a rational, that is a human, soul could exist except with a human body (thus the resurrection of some form of body was necessary if immortality were to be the property of the soul).

Gradually, with the invention of the microscope and the discovery of the circulation of the blood, the biological sciences developed, and different developmental theories became popular, the most bizarre of which was known as preformation, according to which one could see under the new microscope a tiny man, a homunculus, with arms and legs, within each spermatozoon, to which, at conception, a rational soul would be added. A different version of this theory claimed that the little man was to be found not in the sperm but in the ovum (Ovism) (see J. A. Needham, *History of Embryology*, Cambridge University Press 1959, pp. 168ff, and D. A. Jones, *The Soul of the Embryo*, Continuum 2004, pp. 165–166).

For the Roman Catholic Church, the question of how and when the fully human soul became attached to the body, though still of theoretical interest, came to seem less practically important. In 1869, Pope Pius IX, in clarifying which sinners would face automatic excommunication, pronounced that among them were those 'procuring abortion, if successful, without distinguishing whether the foetus was animated or not' (*Constitution Apostolicae Sedis*, 1869). This position was reaffirmed thereafter, as we shall see. In fact abortion at any stage of a pregnancy was pronounced to be a grave sin, and the question of 'animation' or ensoulment could be allowed to drop into the background, a matter for theological dispute, without practical importance. The transition to a more pragmatic, this-worldly view of the human foetus was significant. It showed a church more concerned with what it saw as harm towards an entity actually existing in this world – harm to what was indubitably a living creature, the foetus – and less concerned with God's mysterious workings in creating a soul. At any rate, by 1967 there was never any doubt that the Roman Catholic Church and its members would strongly oppose the Steel Bill on the grounds that human life was sacred at whatever stage of its development, whether ensouled or otherwise.

The use of the word 'sacred' reinforces the religious background to this source of opposition. To describe something as 'sacred' is to invest it with an air of the supernatural, to give it a mysterious value above the value we may attach to the merely profane. Nevertheless, those who in the course of these debates made use of the principle of the Sanctity of Life for the most part denied that they did so because they were Roman Catholics, although they did not deny that they were in fact members of the Church. And this leads to the difficulty that will become familiar in the following three chapters. It is very hard to distinguish those whose arguments and votes were determined by their religion from those whose position was a purely moral one which, as it were, just happened to be in accordance with the teaching of the Church. The Church itself would deny that this was a difficulty. The distinction between religion and morality would be a false one. God, and the Church that gives expression to His commands, is the source of and the ultimate authority on morality. If you want to know how you should vote on the Abortion Bill, find out the official position of the Church. If you are a good Catholic, you will of course consult your conscience – that is, your own sense of what it is wrong or right to do – but your conscience, if properly taught and properly consulted, will come up with the same answer that the Church would give. Consulting a priest is the equivalent of properly consulting your conscience. (Both Catholics and Protestants can therefore subscribe to the Lutheran belief that the conscience is the voice of God speaking within us; but the sense of this belief is very different for each.) It is only when practising Catholics find some part of the teaching of the Church morally objectionable (most commonly perhaps over the use of contraceptives) that they find themselves in the uneasy position of having to make a distinction between religion and morality. And the general coincidence of religion and morality, as we shall see, is not greatly different for those who are members of other Christian Churches. It is taken for granted by many Christians that religion is the source of morality, or that the main point or purpose of religion is to provide moral certainties, a view shared by many who are not religious themselves.

Long before Christianity, Plato put into the mouth of Socrates the question whether something is right because the gods command it or whether the gods command something because it is right. In the Commons Second Reading debate on abortion, one Roman Catholic MP, Norman St John Stevas (now Lord Stevas) seemed to contemplate the same question, and to answer it in favour of the priority of what is right. He said:

'The Bill is fundamentally flawed because it rests upon the denial of the sacred character ... of human life. The principle was recently reaffirmed by the House when it voted for the abolition of the death penalty. This principle is not one dependent on the recondite speculations of scholastic theologians as to when the soul does or does not enter the body, because nobody can know that. It rests upon the moral principle, all but universally accepted, that human life has an intrinsic value in itself and that innocent human life should never be taken.' (*Hansard*, 22 July 1966)

The implication of this reversal of roles, a shared morality having priority over the teachings of the Church, are profound, and will be considered later, but were, unsurprisingly, not pursued in the debate.

In the House of Lords, the following year, though the Duke of Norfolk, the senior Catholic spokesman, did not take part, the Earl of Longford, an enthusiastic Catholic convert, spoke somewhat confusingly about the relation between the doctrines of the Church and individual conscience, confessing that he could imagine circumstances in which the life of the unborn child might have to be sacrificed to that of the mother, as a matter of conscience (but in fact this was also the position of the Church).

He assured the House that they did not have to choose between the Catholic view of abortion and that of the rest. 'There is no doubt that if we were forced to take that decision, a relatively small proportion of the House would take the Roman Catholic view.' Instead, he said, 'we have a solemn choice today' and must consider it 'in the light of the best and most enlightened contemporary opinion'. This was the choice between, on the one hand, upholding the principle of the sanctity of human life, in defence of which he called upon '2,000 years of Christian tradition' and, on the other hand, abandoning this principle. (*Hansard* HL, 19 July 1967). Lord Longford thus drew a distinction between the Christian tradition and the specific doctrines of the Roman Catholic Church, both equally upholding the doctrine of the sanctity of human foetal life. So was his an argument based on religion or was it not? I think his repeated invocation of the concept of sanctity shows that, though subject to the questioning of individual conscience, his judgement was a religious judgement. But perhaps a better way to characterise it is as the judgement of one who genuinely could not distinguish moral (or conscientious) arguments from those based on faith.

Immediately after the Earl of Longford's speech, Lord Soper, a prominent leader of nonconformist Christianity, a profoundly religious man, and recognised as such by all denominations of the Christian Church, rose to defend the Steel Bill, including its 'social clause' that would permit abortion not just to save a woman's life or health, but to save her from harming herself and her whole family if the pregnancy continued. Lord Soper's arguments, in this part of his speech, were entirely based on compassion – that most central of Christian virtues – and he cited specific cases with which he was familiar: that of a pregnant sixteen-year-old child, the victim of rape, terrified literally out of her wits by what had happened and was happening to her; and that of a poor Irish woman, exhorted by her priest to regard her eighth pregnancy as a blessing, who said: 'I wish to God I knew as little about it as he does.' Lord Soper argued that the operation of the social clause – deciding, that is, that the social harm of the pregnancy's continuing outweighed the value of the foetal life – was tantamount to 'ordaining' the doctors to whom it fell to make the decision, giving them not merely medical but also moral authority (the same argument that was used by Lord Brock to oppose the Bill). It would make the medical profession 'the custodians of the sacred mysteries as well as the medical mysteries' (*Hansard* HL, 10 July 1967, p. 39) and this might prove an impossible burden for them to take up. He therefore threw into the ring, but did not pursue the idea, that the logical outcome of the proposed reform would be abortion by consent, or abortion on demand. Moving on to what he called the theological arguments about when the soul appears, he said that he would 'borrow the language of linguistic philosophers, and suggest that this is the wrong question to ask'. He confessed to never having been impressed by the idea of 'instant life, like instant coffee'. 'There is no instant method of distinguishing at one point or another what is existence and what is non-existence. The whole thing is a process.' And he concluded that it was impudent of us to rest the case for the sacrosanct nature of foetal life on what was a medieval philosophy.

Perhaps what Lord Soper's remarkable speech teaches us is the complexity of the relation between religious belief, moral evaluation and theology. We may distinguish religious belief, which may in turn inform the believer's whole value system and all his moral thinking, on the one hand, from theology on the other. It is from theological dogma that the doctrine of the 'sanctity' of human life from the moment of conception derives. 'Sanctity' may thus be distinguished from 'Value', in this context an essentially moral concept (though not of course always so).

This becomes clearer when we turn to the next pieces of legislation to be considered, those concerned with research using human embryos. The new clarity derives from the fact that, while there has been a long tradition, at least from Aristotle's time, of the value of the developing human foetus in its mother's womb, there was not and could not have been any tradition of the value of a live human embryo existing outside a woman's body, since such a thing had never existed until 1978. The question of the value of such lives was therefore wholly new, and the 'sanctity of life' had to be considered afresh in the light of the new phenomenon.

In the 1980s, it was rightly held that research using live human embryos was essential in order to improve the then-new technique for remedying some kinds of infertility, *In Vitro* fertilisation (IVF). Embryo research also seemed increasingly to promise great advances towards the elimination of monogenetic inherited disease, leading to the possibility of removing or manipulating faulty genes in an embryo *in vitro*, or even *in vivo* (a goal that has so far proved elusive). In any case, using an embryo for the purposes of research involved its destruction thereafter, since the risk of its having been damaged during the procedure would be too great to allow it to be placed in a woman's uterus. Research could therefore be equated with the deliberate killing of a live human embryo. Hence the fierce opposition to it from the same people who were opposed to abortion.

The first 'test-tube baby' was born in 1978, after the ovum extracted from a woman had been fertilised with her partner's sperm in a dish, and reinserted into her uterus. This successful birth followed numerous failed attempts, and even after the first success, most reinserted embryos failed to implant in the wall of the uterus, so that no pregnancy was achieved. By the mid-1980s, though several hundred babies had been born by IVF, the success rate was under 10 per cent. If the procedure was to be offered routinely as a remedy for infertility, continued research on every aspect of it was needed, including the composition and temperature of the fluid in which fertilisation could best take place. Any embryos used for such research, if they did not die naturally in the course of the procedures, must be destroyed. The embryos to be used in the research could either be left over from actual fertilisation procedures (for more than one egg was routinely fertilised *in vitro*, and the best resulting embryos inserted in the uterus or frozen for future use, the rest discarded) or, more controversially, they could be specially created for research, using donated eggs and sperm.

After the first successful IVF birth in 1978, there was huge excitement in the media, some people welcoming this as a miracle for the infertile, others regarding it as yet further evidence of the arrogance of scientists, taking to themselves the role of the creator, God. The latter view was reinforced by an unfortunate television programme which showed Mr Patrick Steptoe, the surgeon who, with Dr Bob Edwards, had been responsible for the first live embryo to be produced in the laboratory, peering through his microscope and exclaiming 'we've created life'. But whatever the view of the moralists, infertile couples were eagerly signing up for treatment, and it was clear that IVF would either have to be accepted (suitably regulated) or prohibited by law. However, the issues were too complex and too controversial for the immediate drafting of a Bill; so the Committee of Inquiry into Human Fertilisation and Embryology was set up in 1982 to examine all the problems, as far as they might be foreseen, and to advise the government on possible legislation. The Committee reported to the Minister of Social Security (Norman Fowler, later Lord Fowler) in the summer of 1984.

In the following year, long before the Government had finished considering and consulting on the findings of the Committee of Inquiry, and before it was ready to start drafting a Bill, Enoch Powell, the Member of Parliament for South Down, introduced a Private Member's Bill named the Unborn Children (Protection)

Bill, which had its Second Reading in February 1985. This was his opening statement in the debate: 'The Bill has a single and simple purpose. It is to render it unlawful for a human embryo created by *in vitro* fertilisation to be used as the subject of experiment or, indeed, in any other way or for any other purpose except to enable a woman to bear a child' (*Hansard*, 15 February 1985). According to the provisions of this Bill, only a single egg might be fertilised *in vitro*, and only for a specific woman, who would have to apply to take part in the procedure to the Secretary of State, after being vetted by two doctors as suitable. If she did not become pregnant within four months of having the first single embryo inserted into her uterus, she might gain a two-month extension of the permission, but if she failed to become pregnant after six months and still wanted to try for a child she would have to start all over again with a new application to the Secretary of State. There was no proposed limit to the number of times the poor woman might apply.

Mr Powell was, perhaps forgivably, ignorant of how absurd his six-month time limit was, and of the need to fertilise more eggs than one in each IVF cycle in order to have the best chance of success. Moreover, he graciously allowed that doctors might use new and untried procedures as long as their intention was to enable a woman to have a baby ; and this of course entailed that while an embryo was to be protected from being used as a research object, the woman herself was allowed to be so used, as the subject of 'untried' treatment.

The Bill was thus nonsensical. What is of more interest, however, is the reason Mr Powell gave to support his proposed prohibition of embryo research. He said:

'The question may now be asked: why should a bill be brought forward to forbid the use of a human embryo from becoming the subject of experiment? If I may, I should like to answer that question in personal terms. When I first read the Warnock report (The Report of the Com-

24

mittee of Inquiry into Human Fertilization and Embryology 1984) I had a sense of revulsion and repugnance, deep and instinctive towards the proposition that a thing, however it may be defined of which the sole purpose or object is that it may be a human life, should be subjected to experiment to its destruction for the purpose of the acquisition of knowledge.'

Mr Powell went on to deny that he appeals to any abstract principle of when an embryo becomes a human being, stating that that is unanswerable, 'because it goes to the heart of the great unanswerable question, What is Man?' Nor did he rely on religious arguments, though he acknowledged that many of his supporters did so rely. He did not deny, either, that useful medical knowledge could be gained by research using human embryos. Instead he asked the House to make a choice and to 'decide that the moral, social and human cost of that information being obtained in a way that outrages the instincts of so many is too great a price to pay'. The basis of the argument was thus 'outrage of the instincts' of many people (the same basis, incidentally, as that used by Lord Justice Devlin in 1967 against the legalisation of homosexual practice between consenting men: the horror and disgust of the 'man on the Clapham Omnibus').

His argument was taken up by many MPs who simply appealed to the principle of the sanctity of life. However, Mr Campbell-Savours (later Lord Campbell-Savours), in supporting the Bill, and supporting it on grounds of the sanctity of life, nevertheless was alone in making the point that this was not a sufficient argument in a legislative context. He said:

'A Christian need do no more than pronounce his article of faith … For those of us who subscribe to such views, they may be sufficient justification for supporting the Bill. But I do not believe that that approach, without the intellectual base that requires deliberation and evaluation of its merits, is sufficient to convince the House. Therefore it is not a basis on which an hon. Member could make up his or her mind during the debate.'

He concluded that a reason for supporting the Bill, indeed a justification for any legislation at all on the issue, must be found that will 'convince the atheist'. And he ended by tentatively suggesting that such a reason might be that embryos used for research would feel pain. This would provide a respectable Utilitarian argument that would convince atheists to support the Powell Bill.

It is remarkable that neither Mr Campbell-Savours nor anyone else in this debate took seriously the recommendation of the Committee of Inquiry that there should be a 14-day limit on the length of time after it had come into being that the embryo might be kept alive in the laboratory, and used for research; it was, I suppose, simply assumed that such a limiting regulation would be immediately or gradually breached. In fact the time limitation became part of the law in 1990, with a penalty of ten years' imprisonment attached as a sanction, and as far as I know has not been breached. Of course if Mr Campbell-Savours had taken that suggested limitation seriously he would have known that his tentative argument that might convince the atheists would have no force, admirable though I believe it was to see the necessity of such an argument. For before 14 days from fertilisation, the cells of the embryo are not differentiated, and it has not even the beginnings of a central nervous system, so its feeling anything at all, pain or pleasure, is out of the question. But perhaps most people did not notice the 14-day limit proposed by the report because it was a limit irrelevant to those like Enoch Powell himself who held that the life of any human embryo at whatever stage of development was sacred.

Fortunately, though Enoch Powell's Bill was voted a Second Reading by a large majority, it did not proceed, and the Government showed no inclination to encourage it. And so we move on to 1989/90, when the Human Fertilisation and Embryology Bill was passed and became law.

From the evidence, both written and oral, that it received, as well as from its own internal discussions, the Committee of

Inquiry that I chaired had realised that if it were to advise ministers that IVF should be permitted, it was essential to find a way to make continued research acceptable to Parliament and the public, and that this would be its most difficult task. Indeed, Enoch Powell's attempted Bill showed that this was true. There were some of those who gave evidence to the Committee who opposed the IVF procedure altogether. This was because it was vaguely thought to be unnatural, or a usurpation of God's role, or, more specifically, because the procedure involved masturbation which was held by the Roman Catholic Church to be a sin, even if its purpose was to produce life. However, most of those who were hostile to or suspicious of IVF held, like Enoch Powell, that the procedure was not intrinsically wrong, as long as it did not involve either the immediate destruction of embryos that were not wanted for implantation ('surplus embryos') or research using live embryos and their subsequent destruction. I have already explained that this was not a tenable or realistic position, and the Committee had to find a way to undermine it. We addressed the question in chapter 11 of the report. We argued there that the question 'when does human life begin?', upon the answer to which was supposed to turn the answer to the further question of whether research, and the deliberate destruction of embryos, should be permitted, was not, as it appeared, a question of fact, but a question of value. It was a question that could be decided by Parliament, not, as some suggested, by further scientific research. (Some people even proposed that there should be a moratorium on all research until such time as scientists had discovered when human life began.) But, as Lord Soper had suggested in a different context, this was a case where, in the jargon of 1950s philosophy, the wrong question was being asked. Paragraph 11.9 of the report reads: 'we have considered what status ought to be accorded to the human embryo, and the answer we give must necessarily be in terms of ethical or moral principles.' I did not realise at the

the laboratory, instead of in the female fallopian tube.' At what point in the development of an individual human life does it become so valuable that it should not be sacrificed, even for the sake of the good that might come from the research that would lead to its destruction? Everyone agreed that no child who had been born should be so sacrificed, but there agreement ended.

It must be remembered that even in the 1980s, most people, unless they were biological scientists, were profoundly ignorant of the facts of embryonic development. The pro-life lobby, as hostile to research using human embryos as they were to abortion, took as their logo an image of a human foetus, curled up in the womb. The name of Enoch Powell's Bill, The Unborn Child (Protection) Bill was misleading. The Duke of Norfolk, who, as senior Roman Catholic in the House of Lords, felt he must acquaint himself with the facts about IVF, to his great credit went to visit Robert Winston's fertility clinic in the Hammersmith Hospital, and I remember his accosting me in the corridor of the House, and taking me into the dining room for a cup of tea (carefully guiding me to the table under the picture of his Roman Catholic ancestor being first admitted to Parliament), and there, and on many subsequent days, he explained how he had changed his mind about embryo research. He had thought an embryo was visibly a baby. He had learned from Robert Winston, with the help of a microscope, that in the days after conception the embryo was invisible to the naked eye; and he had learned how the cells multiply and differentiate into different kinds of cells until on about the fifteenth day a cluster of cells begins to appear in the centre of the group of cells, the Primitive Streak, which will now quite quickly develop into the spinal cord, and the central nervous system. He had become, in fact, like Lord Soper, a developmentalist. He could accept what the Committee of Inquiry had had to learn, most of them, for the first time: that up to 14 days from fertilisation, any cell may become any part of the body, or not any part of the body, but part of the umbilical cord or the after-birth; and that up to that time two embryos may split off from each other as identical twins, with two spinal cords. He was prepared, that is, to accept what we had recommended: that up to 14 days from fertilisation embryos need not, indeed could not, be treated as individual complete human persons, but might be regarded as clusters of human cells, and, as such, used for research. It was a steep conceptual learning curve for him, as it had been for the non-scientific members of the Committee, he having been taught by the great human embryologist, Lord Winston, we by the equally great mammalian physiologist, Professor Anne McLaren, a member of the committee and a brilliant teacher.

Sadly, it must be recorded that the Duke's conversion was short-lived. Our conversations took place in 1986, soon after I joined the House of Lords and two years after the publication of the Committee's report. In March 1987 The Congregation of the Doctrine of the Faith of the Catholic Church published its *Instruction on Respect for Human Life in its Origin and on the Dignity of Human Procreation: Replies to Certain Questions of the Day.* The questions were those concerned with research using human embryos; and the Instruction, though no claim was made to solve the ancient puzzle of the time of ensoulment, nevertheless laid down that

'the Church accepts that the genetic or biological identity of a new human individual begins at fertilization when a zygote (a two-cell embryo) is formed and takes it for granted that this suffices for the presence of a human being … On the basis of an ordinary human understanding of these facts the Church adopts the position of pruden-tial certitude in relation to the presence of individual and personal life once the process of fertilization results in the constitution of a zygote through the union of human egg and sperm.'

Thus the Church again, as it had in 1869, distinguished theoreti-cal or theological questions about ensoulment from an 'ordinary human understanding of the facts'; and though it recognised that an embryo and a foetus and a child were developmentally different, as far as being used for research purposes went, all were equal, with the same ethical status. The Duke and I had our last tea together the day after this Instruction was published, and he said with considerable melancholy that he, a mere soldier, did not know what to think, but knew that he would have to speak up against the Bill to legitimise research, whenever it should come before the House. This it did, at last, in December 1989.

The Bill, starting in the House of Lords, was carried through with extraordinary skill and impeccable impartiality by the then Lord Chancellor, Lord Mackay of Clashfern. The delay between the publication of the report in July 1984 and the introduction of the Bill turned out to be a great advantage. Because of the work of such experts as Robert Winston and Anne McLaren, ignorance began to be dispelled among the general public; and meanwhile more successful pregnancies resulted from IVF, regulated by an Interim Human Fertility and Embryology Authority, which was modelled on the regulative body that the Committee's report had recommended as its first priority. The Interim Authority was a voluntary organisation, consisting of gynaecologists and others, giving up their time, and finding the workload increasingly burdensome. They were therefore strongly urging the Government to get on with the work of drafting a Bill.

The Bill, when it came, had a unique form. On the crucial issue of research, on which the Roman Catholics (including, of course, the good Duke of Norfolk) and others who were 'pro-life' were implacably hostile, there were two alternative clauses on which members of the House of Lords had to vote. One clause prohibited all research using human embryos, the other permitted it for up to 14 days from fertilisation, as the Report of the Committee of Inquiry had recommended. This meant that argument could focus on this clause when it came to be debated, and peers could give a clear yes or no answer about the future of research (and thus in effect the future of IVF in this country), leaving the other clauses, concerned with the regulation of IVF and other forms of infertility treatment, to be debated separately. To me – sitting nervously silent, since I felt I had already had my say in the report, and could add nothing to that – there seemed to be two crucial speeches that carried the Bill through, to be sent on to the Commons. The first was the intervention of Lord Walton of Detchant, a recently retired neurosurgeon, and new to the House, who spoke with passion on the value of embryonic research for finding remedies for such diseases as Duchenne's Muscular Dystrophy, his own speciality. He spoke not only as a doctor, but as a Lay Reader in the Methodist Church.

The other was the intervention of the then Archbishop of York, John Habgood, once an academic biologist, who spoke for the gradualism of biological scientists, whether they were concerned with the evolution of species or the development of an individual embryo. He said, 'It seems strange to a biologist that all the weight of moral argument should be placed on one definable moment at the beginning', and he ended his speech with the words: 'Christians are no more required to believe that humanness is created in an instant than we are required to believe in the historical existence of Adam and Eve' (Later in the debate an aged peer who was sitting next to me whispered, 'no Christian could have anything to do with this stuff', and I ventured to ask 'what about the Archbishop of York?', to which he replied 'HE'S not a Christian.' No doubt any fundamentalist Christians who heard or read his speech were equally dismissive.)

At any rate, as far as the House of Lords was concerned the Bill was sent on to the Commons with a substantial majority, including the clause permitting research using human embryos, up to 14 days from fertilisation. There was then a time of anxiety, because anti-abortion MPs, thinking they saw a chance to amend the 1967

Abortion Act, added an amendment to the Bill, limiting the lawful availability of abortion. But when this came back again to the House of Lords, the amendment was not allowed. It was irrelevant to the Fertilisation Bill, and, because of time constraints, it threatened the whole Bill, which by now the Government was under considerable pressure to place on the statute book. So in the end, and, I felt, almost miraculously, IVF became lawful, subject to the 14-day restriction on research, and to other regulatory constraints to be finalised by the new Human Fertilisation and Embryology Authority. Since 1990 there have been various fairly minor changes to the Act, but the powers of the Human Fertilisation and Embryology Authority remain in place, as does the crucial 14-day limit on keeping an embryo alive in the laboratory.

The next serious challenge to the sanctity of life came following the birth of the cloned sheep, Dolly, in the Roslin Research Institute, near Edinburgh, in 1997. The nucleus of an egg cell, containing almost all the DNA of the sheep whose egg it was, was taken out and replaced by the nucleus of a mammalian cell from another adult sheep. An electric current was passed through the egg with its new nucleus, which caused it to fuse and develop into an embryo. This embryo was then placed in the uterus of a third sheep, a surrogate mother. Out of 270 experimental pregnancies, only one lamb, Dolly, survived. She was somewhat overweight, and suffered increasingly from arthritis in her legs, but lived to the age of six, approximately middle age for a sheep. Her birth was greeted with extreme alarm.

There were three separate causes for anxiety. The first was that, though research on the cloning of animals had been going on for more than 40 years, it had previously been conducted using amphibians, it being far easier to use animals whose eggs were outside the body. Now that a mammal had been successfully cloned, it was feared that there could eventually be human clones, a thought that aroused intense horror. This would indeed be the beginning of a Brave New World, Aldous Huxley- rather than Shakespeare-style, with armies of worker-clones being produced, to carry out the dirty work uncomplainingly, and ruler-clones to conquer the world. Or successful and vain people would want clones of themselves, so that the future world might benefit from their talents. Others warned that human clones would be deprived of personal identity, and would not be real individual people at all.

The second source of alarm was that mammalian cloning did not require both sperm and egg, but egg alone; so there was no need for male participation in the process. The resulting child would be literally fatherless, not having been brought into existence by conception in the normal way. This seemed to many the most disastrously unnatural of all those phenomena brought about or made possible by new technology.

Third, those who had always been opposed to research using human embryos that resulted in the destruction of the embryo, even when such research increased the chances of successful fertility treatment, raised their fundamental objection again in the new context, pointing especially to the numbers of embryos destroyed in the production of just one viable offspring.

Scientists vainly argued that they were not interested in producing human clones analogous to Dolly the sheep (reproductive cloning). Instead they wanted to pursue the goal of asexual production of human embryos with a view to extracting stem cells from them, which could be differentiated into different kinds of human cells, and perhaps used in the future to renew damaged cells in living subjects. They fully accepted that any research they carried out would be subject to the provision of the Human Fertilisation and Embryology Act (1990) according to which no embryo might be kept alive in the laboratory for more than 14 days, and no embryo used for research might be placed in a woman's uterus. Moreover, the 1990 Act expressly prohibited human cloning, even though, at the time, it was not believed to be possible. It seemed that the Act absolutely prohibited reproductive cloning.

The point of stem cell research was nothing to do with producing new babies. For stem cell scientists, the purpose of the new technology was twofold. First, they wanted to learn more about the early development of the human embryo and the differentiation of cells. Second, as I have said, they would be able to create embryos by cell nuclear transfer, and extract stem cells from them. Embryonic stem cells are totipotent; that is, they have the capacity to develop into any one of the approximately two hundred types of cells that make up the human body. They could thus be induced to develop into, for example, blood or muscle or spinal cord cells, and banks of such cells could be set up, the cells reproducing themselves everlastingly. They could then be used for transplant in cases of severe injury, say to the spinal cord, or of degeneration of an organ due to disease. Once transplanted, they would colonise, reproduce themselves and take over from the damaged cells they were used to replace.

Techniques for inducing adult stem cells to revert to the stage of totipotency ('turning the clock back') are also being developed, and these too will lead to more understanding of how differentiation actually occurs, and how cells may be guided into different channels of differentiation. The great advantage of techniques using adult cells would be, first, that no embryos need be used, whether the outcome of *in vitro* fertilisation or cell nuclear replacement; and second, that a patient could use a cell from his or her own body, to be transformed into the replacement cell that the injury or disease demanded, so there would be no danger of rejection. The use of cell transplant for the overcoming of disease or injury, known as therapeutic cloning, is widely seen as one of the most exciting future advances in medicine. (For example, it is thought that within a few years a patient's own cells, taken from hair or skin, may be transplanted into the eye to overcome an extremely common disease, Age-Related Macular Degeneration, a development that would transform the life of many elderly people.)

With a view to developing this kind of therapy, early in 2001 Parliament introduced regulations that permitted the use of embryos for research the purpose of which was not confined to the remedying of infertility, as had been laid down in the 1990 Act. However, later in the same year, a member of the pro-life group, convinced that once the production of embryos by cell nuclear replacement had been allowed human reproductive cloning would follow, demanded a judgment from the High Court as to whether the Human Fertilisation and Embryology Act (1990) did actually make human reproductive cloning unlawful. In a surprising judgment, Lord Justice Crane decided that it did not. In the relevant part of the Act, where the insertion of a cloned embryo into a woman's uterus is prohibited, it refers to 'live embryos, where fertilization is complete'; but, he ruled, this cannot be taken to cover embryos that have been produced by nuclear transfer, since they have never undergone fertilisation. In fact, he judged, they were not embryos at all (though he later withdrew this eccentric part of the judgment). Therefore it looked as if cloning a human being the way Dolly had been cloned would after all be lawful under the 1990 Act.

Parliament was thrown into panic. At once, an Italian doctor called Professor Antonori, already notorious for providing IVF treatment for post-menopausal women, promised to come over to England, where, he said, he had 200 women willing to act as surrogate mothers, and there would be a cloned baby within a year. In an almost unconstitutionally short time an Act reached the statute book the sole clause of which was the prohibiting of Human Cloning. It was a minor triumph for the religious and pro-life lobby. And it could be argued that, even if hastily introduced, it did no harm, though personally I can think of cases, say of a man's total inability to produce sperm, where cloning might be a solution to a couple's infertility. But then, I do not share the widespread horror of clones that many people express (though they do not seem to mind identical twins, who in fact have entirely the same DNA, while clones would share only about 90 per cent, some small amount being contained in the membrane surrounding the denucleated donor egg).

Many other animals have been cloned since Dolly, some having been genetically manipulated at the stage when the nucleus of an egg has been transferred to a denucleated egg, in order to produce animals whose cells, or even organs, might be used for human transplant; and human embryonic stem cell research is now permitted by law in the UK. Though some Roman Catholics, especially Lord Alton of Liverpool, repeatedly urge that adult stem cells or stem cells from the umbilical cord should be used instead of embryonic stem cells, the most they have gained is the concession that research should continue using all types of stem cell, including embryonic (the other types are difficult to acquire, and not so versatile, since they can differentiate into only a few types of cell). Lord Alton's argument is based on the respect owed to human life in the embryo, regardless of how that embryo comes into existence; and he cites the numbers of embryos destroyed in research programmes to back up his argument. But there is a sense in which, if to destroy an early embryo is wrong, then to destroy even one is wrong. It is not necessarily a hundred times more wrong to destroy a hundred, at least so it seems to me. But this is to suppose a crucial difference between embryos and people (which Lord Alton does not allow). For it seems *prima facie* true that it is a hundred times worse to kill a hundred people than one (though even this must depend on the motive and circumstances).

In any case, behind all the opposition to embryonic stem cell research there lies something other than the mere calculation of numbers of embryos destroyed. It is doubtful whether many people, despite the instructions from the Vatican, really believe in their heart that the death of a two- or four-cell zygote is comparable to the death of a child who has been born. They need only reflect on the extraordinary luck that is required for such an embryo, conceived in the natural way, to implant in the uterus and become a baby, the huge wastage of embryos that Nature permits, to doubt whether there is really any comparison. Would God allow so many souls to be lost? I believe that their opposition is based rather on a general sense that producing human embryos by a means other than human fertilisation is unnatural and therefore wrong. Many people had felt the same about IVF, at the beginning, but at least in that procedure spermatozoon and egg are brought together to fuse, albeit outside the body. It was the possibility of asexual reproduction in the years following the birth of Dolly the sheep that seemed so wholly contrary to nature.

David Hume, when looking for the 'general principles upon which our notion of morals might be founded', raised the question whether they were derived from Nature. In that case something unnatural would be morally wrong. But he went on to say that, to assert this connection, we would need to know how 'Nature' is to be understood, 'than which', he said, 'there is no word more ambiguous and equivocal'. It is difficult to find a definition of the Natural that does not already contain an evaluative element, entailing that the unnatural is worse than the natural. We tend, like Rousseau, to believe that the natural is good, and that nothing but corruption comes from man-made changes, producing thereby the artificial. To do what is contrary to Nature is *wrongfully* to intervene in the natural order of things. Thus people who think that some surgical operations, such as giving someone a pacemaker, are good, while others, such as breast enhancement, are bad, are liable to describe the latter but not the former as unnatural. And there are many agricultural and horticultural interventions where the use of 'unnatural' is equally selective.

The idea of Nature's Order is closely linked with the idea of what God has ordained. And in some respects the development of science, and the Darwinian idea of biological gradualism, seems hardly to have touched the taken-for-granted view of popular, as opposed to scientific, culture. Thus, when pigs were first cloned and the piglets genetically modified so that their organs might be used in human transplant, there was widespread outrage. This was to cross the species boundary, creating hybrid monsters. One could say that it was contrary to God's creation of separate species of animals, preserved in their pairs, according to Genesis 6–8, in Noah's Ark during the Great Flood. One could equally say that it fell foul of Nature's distinction between one species and another. Yet we know, since the discovery of DNA, how genetically similar animals are to each other, how large a proportion of our genes we share not only with the higher apes, but with the fruit-fly. Some animals are more intelligent than others, but we are not divided from any by the huge barriers, differences of kind, that used to be supposed. We swing between thinking that the laws of Nature cannot be breached to thinking that they ought not to be breached. No wonder Hume found the word 'Nature' equivocal.

And so it is that, once again, we come up against the difficulty of separating religious from non-religious beliefs. For example, in his Reith Lecture delivered in 2001 the Prince of Wales, speaking against the genetic modification of crops, said: 'It is because of our inability or refusal to accept the existence of a Guiding Hand that nature has come to be regarded as a system that can be engineered for our own convenience and in which anything that happens can be fixed by technology and human ingenuity.' It is easy to slip into the language of theology when considering what we regard as undue human interventions in the natural course of events: the Guiding Hand may be the hand of God or of Nature herself. '*Deus sive Natura*' in the atheist Spinoza's words; either may seem equally sacrosanct. Many people feel that asexual reproduction, for purposes of therapeutic cloning, however great its potential benefits, is something simply too far removed from what God or Nature have laid down to be tolerable, and this is the deep source of their unease.

CHAPTER TWO

Life, Death and Authority:
A Legislative History – Part Two

The very last case to be heard by the Law Lords, sitting, according to tradition, wigged and robed in the House of Lords, was the appeal by a young woman called Debbie Purdey to be given clarification of the law concerning assisted suicide. She was suffering from Multiple Sclerosis and wanted an assurance that if at some time in the future she asked her husband to take her to Zurich, where she could lawfully be provided with a lethal dose, he would not be prosecuted on his return to the UK. Aiding and abetting suicide is a criminal offence under the Suicide Act (1961), and there would undoubtedly be enough evidence to convict if he came to trial, having accompanied her to Switzerland with the express intention that she should die at the hands of a Swiss doctor. Yet within the previous few years, over a hundred British citizens had gone, with relatives to help them, on the journey to the organisation called Dignitas, which painlessly kills those who genuinely want to die; and none of those who had accompanied these death-seekers had been prosecuted on their return. Though the police had questioned them and referred their cases to the Director of Public Prosecutions, in each case he had concluded that it would not be in the public interest to proceed with a prosecution. This, of course, gave no clue to the grounds of his decision, nor to whether he might decide differently in future. On 23 July 2009, the Law Lords, as their last judgment before being transformed into the Supreme Court – stripped of their robes and moved across Parliament Square – found that the DPP must clearly set out the criteria that he would use to decide whether to prosecute those who aided and abetted suicide under a foreign legislature. On 23 September, draft guidelines were published in which the DDP set out his position. Assisting suicide would remain a criminal offence (unless Parliament should one day decide to change the law). But there would probably be no prosecution if the person seeking death could be shown to be terminally or incurably ill, and to have consistently asked for help to die, and if the person giving the assistance did not stand to gain financially or in any other way from the death (this, one would think, would be a difficult condition to satisfy). Such considerations would be taken into account whether the suicide occurred in the UK or abroad. But it would still rest with the DPP to decide whether or not the criteria had been satisfied. At the time of writing, these guidelines are out for consultation. They have caused considerable dissatisfaction in that they seem to do no more than reaffirm the present state of the law, without giving the certainty that is sought. They certainly give no protection to doctors or nurses who might hasten the death of a patient who was dying. But the DPP was right to argue that it was not for him to change the law. That must be for Parliament. At any rate, it was a kind of victory for Debbie Purdey, and a small step in the direction of decriminalising assisted death for those who are terminally or incurably ill, and who want to be relieved from their suffering.

There had already been an attempt to change the 1961 Suicide Act, in the House of Lords. A few days before the Law Lords reached their decision, Lord Falconer, the last Lord Chancellor before the abolition of the office, and now returned to the Labour back benches, brought forward an amendment to the Coroners and Justice Bill, at the time going through the House of Lords, that would have been a larger step towards decriminalisation. He proposed a clause that would exempt from the provisions of the Act anyone helping another to go to die under a legislature where assisted suicide or euthanasia was permitted. He, like Debbie Purdy herself, wanted clarification of the law, and of the DPP's position. However, the amendment was voted down by a substantial majority of the House. Some opposed it on the grounds that the law was perfectly clear already: assisting suicide was a criminal offence and that was the end of it, whatever the DPP might choose to do. Others argued that Lord Falconer's amendment was a fraud. It might be put forward as a mere quest for clarification, but in reality it was intended as the first move in a campaign to legalise assisted dying. Feelings ran high, as was natural in a debate so obviously concerned with matters of life and death, lying at the heart of morality, and central also to religious belief.

This, then, is the question to which I turn in this chapter. What arguments are relevant to the decision whether some form of assisted dying should be made lawful? If someone is terminally ill, or suffering acutely from an incurable condition, and if that person expresses a serious and settled wish to die, ought the law to be so changed as to permit assistance? No one could doubt that this is a question of morals as well as of law, and one in which religious belief is deeply concerned. How, then, is it to be settled?

As the law stands, deliberately to bring about someone's death, even when that person has begged to die, is murder, an offence that, since the abolition of the death penalty, has carried a mandatory life sentence, whatever the motives or circumstances of the crime. Thus someone who, let us say, out of love and pity, reluctantly accedes to the requests of his spouse and suffocates her, is put in the same category of offender as a deliberately sadistic murderer, or someone who kills in the course of armed robbery. All are subject to the same mandatory life sentence. However, this is a somewhat absurd position, for though the judge who finds someone guilty of murder is obliged to pass a so-called life sentence, it is only in a very few cases that this means that convicted murderers will stay in prison all their life. Their discharge, after perhaps a few years, will depend on the decision of the parole board, which may deem them to be no danger to the public, though it is true that they may be returned to prison at any time after their release. But those who assist a loved one to die in response to a repeated request to do so will be most unlikely to kill again, or to constitute any sort of danger to the public, so remaining under the threat of a possible return to prison seems a totally inappropriate part of the punishment.

On 26 October 2009, Lord Lloyd of Berwick, a former Lord of Appeal and former president of the Law Society, proposed an amendment to the Coroners and Justice Bill that would have given a judge in a murder trial the option of allowing the jury to decide whether in the case before them they might wish to argue that there had been extenuating circumstances in a particular murder, and if they did so the judge might then, if he so pleased, pass a sentence short of a life sentence. This would differentiate mercy killing, or killing under extreme provocation, from brutal or sadistic murder; and because it would be for the jury to make the plea of extenuating circumstances, the outcome would reflect the views of the general public, not of the judge alone. However, neither the Government nor the official opposition would support this amendment, though all those who spoke in the debate, most of them lawyers and including a bishop, were in favour of it. No serious arguments were brought against it; and the suspicion must remain that neither of the two main parties was prepared to risk being seen as 'soft on crime' and consequently reviled by the press. So, sadly, this humane and reasonable change will not, or not yet, come about, prevented by purely political, not

moral considerations. Let us, then, return to the moral considerations in questions of assisted dying.

Since 1961, suicide has not been a crime, but aiding and abetting suicide is a criminal offence, carrying a maximum sentence
of 14 years' imprisonment. I have written at length elsewhere
about the moral aspects of this law and the law on homicide as it
affects so-called mercy killing (see Mary Warnock and Elisabeth
MacDonald, *Easeful Death: Is there a Case for Assisted Dying?*,
Oxford University Press 2008). In this chapter I will try to concentrate, not so much on the rights and wrongs of assisted dying
as on the nature of the arguments that are commonly used, for
and against a change in the law. Since the law of homicide is at
the very centre of the criminal law, and murder is the most
heinous of criminal offences, to speak of 'the arguments' here
must mean to speak of arguments in the context of legislation,
either those used in Parliament itself, or those used by commen-
tators debating about what Parliament ought to do. Even more
obviously than over the death of embryos and foetuses, the law
must rule over the deliberate killing of people who have been
born. But, as I have already said, the issue is moral as well as legal;
indeed there can be no more central and difficult question for
moralists and moral philosophers than whether it may be justifiable in certain circumstances to take another person's life, or
help them to take their own. The question of whether the law
should be changed follows and depends on the answer to that
moral question.

In the UK a good deal of parliamentary time since the beginning of the century has been devoted to questions about euthanasia and assisted suicide. Lord Joffe, a distinguished human rights
lawyer, has made four attempts (in 2003, 2004, 2005 and 2006) to
get a Private Member's Bill permitting assisted death in certain
strictly defined circumstances through the House of Lords, and
so, through its various stages, onto the statute book, but all have

failed. Before his last attempt, a House of Lords Select Committee was set up, under the chairmanship of Lord Mackay of Clashfern, to examine the issues, and the Committee's published report and the evidence they took from both individuals and institutions give an exceptionally detailed insight into the legal, moral and religious arguments deployed on both sides of the debate.

The Select Committee held that, in considering the case for and against legalising assisted dying, the difficulty lay in a conflict between two principles – the principle of the sanctity of human life and that of autonomy – both of which were adopted by nearly all the protagonists, but which were accorded different priorities. They structured their report around this clash of principles. The principle of human autonomy, and in this context, of specifically patient autonomy, is a wholly secular principle, often nowadays connected with the concept of human rights. The principle of the sanctity of life, on the other hand, is predominantly, though not exclusively, a religious argument. Thus at the outset, the Select Committee seemed to be on the brink of distinguishing morality from religion as the basis for possible legislation. I shall return to the sanctity of life, already mentioned in the previous chapter, in due course. But first let us consider autonomy.

The principle of autonomy, widely regarded as a cornerstone of modern medical ethics, requires that patients should decide whether a course of treatment is acceptable to them or not. No medical intervention may take place without the patient's informed consent; otherwise the doctor is guilty of assault (though it is allowed that there will be exceptions to this in cases of emergency). Moreover, a patient is entitled by law to refuse treatment, even if the doctor thinks it would be in his or her best interest to have it.

So far, then, it looks as though there is indeed a principle of patient autonomy that doctors are obliged to respect. Student doctors in their now compulsory ethics courses are taught this principle, and some are taught that it is the cardinal principle of medical ethics. Many ethics teachers, wishing no doubt to give the principle a respectable and venerable pedigree, derive it not from the fear that a doctor may be sued for assault, if he or she intervenes without consent, but from a wider more philosophical principle, held to be at the heart of morality itself, namely that every human being equally should be treated as a free and rational agent, able to make responsible choices, and in charge of their own lives. This central emphasis on respect for the choice-making abilities of others is often ascribed (a bit loosely) to the great system-builder of the mid-eighteenth century, Immanuel Kant. He held that the only thing that could be *morally* good in the world was the good will. There could be other good things, like good wine or good music, but these goods had nothing to do with morality, only with pleasure. The good will was the name Kant gave to the ability common and unique to human beings of acting from a rational calculation of what it is one's duty to do. He held this view because, like many of his contemporaries, he was dazzled by the apparent consequences of Newtonian physics, which showed that every aspect of the universe is governed by immutable physical laws. Since human beings are part of the physical universe, they too might be expected to behave according to the same laws, and the concept of morality would drop away. No one could make choices, either good or bad, nor could they be held personally responsible for what they did. Research would show that what they did was inevitable, given the circumstances they were in; and similarly what they would do in the future could be predicted like the behaviour of matter. There could be no morality. However, Kant argued that we know morality exists, because we recognise immediately when we are faced with something that morally we must or must not do. So he sought to save morality, by arguing that, alone among creatures, human beings are possessed of reason. It is according to practical reason that they can after all determine their own behaviour and

into account as far as possible in deciding what to do. Though the ideal of treating everyone as a free individual capable of making his or her own decisions and entitled to do so may be well enough, we know that in practice a lot of our moral agonising may focus on precisely the question to what extent they are actually capable of doing so, and to what extent we must sometimes decide for them. Moreover, in real life the law of the land limits individual autonomy at every turn. We cannot choose to drive a car if we are drunk, or drive it uninsured, or bring up our children without education. Even within medicine, a patient cannot choose precisely what treatment he or she is to receive; nor expect their wishes to outweigh a clinician's superior knowledge in every case. Nor can one demand treatment that one's doctor thinks will be futile, especially if receiving it deprives another patient who would benefit more. The principle of autonomy is here outweighed by the principle of justice, often taught as another central principle of medical ethics. Autonomy cannot be without limits.

Yet it can be argued that, even if this is true and autonomy has limits, in medicine, at least, patient autonomy is an important principle, indeed paramount, because of the position of power that doctors occupy relative to their patients. Doctors have knowledge that the patient does not share; they have access to the drugs and equipment that they may or may not choose to use; they, traditionally, have been the authority, not only in virtue of their knowledge, but in the sense that they have been the people in command, or the ones to give orders. Because of the evils that are seen to reside in such paternalism, it may be held that, in an age when we insist on equality of rights, the principle of autonomy is especially important in the medical field. Does this entail that everyone has the right to choose to die, if that is what they wish? Can bringing death to a patient who longs for an end to suffering ever be deemed to be the only way in which his or her autonomy can be respected, and therefore the doctor's duty? This is the question on which opinions, and principles, divide.

Let us look at a real example, a case in some ways like that of Ms Purdey, with whom this chapter started. In 2002, Diane Pretty, who suffered from Motor Neurone disease, and, being paralysed, was incapable of committing suicide without assistance, sought an assurance from the Director of Public Prosecutions that her husband would be exempt from prosecution under the Suicide Act (1961) if, at a time of her choosing, she sought his help to end her life. The DPP refused her request, which was likewise turned down by the High Court. She took her case to the Court of Human Rights at Strasbourg, where her claim was also disallowed (*Pretty v United Kingdom* (application 2346/02) [2002] 2 FLR 45). This court explicitly ruled that, though there was a human right to life, there was no such right to death. Thus, those who rely on the principle of autonomy to support their supposed right to choose death are claiming that there ought to be such a right, though currently there is not, or that, according to some higher law than the present law, there already is such a right, which ought to be recognised by the courts; an inalienable human right which the court at Strasbourg denied. Such claims against current laws have always been made, and they are essentially moral claims. I shall return to the question of criticising the law according to moral standards in the next chapter. Meanwhile, the very nature of the widely publicised dispute over Diane Pretty's appeal (and there have been many other similar cases in the USA and elsewhere) shows that the principle of autonomy on which she was relying does not obviously trump every other consideration; and we must now turn to that other guiding principle with which it is said to conflict: that of the sanctity of life.

I argued in the last chapter that the belief that human life is sacred, and the consequent adoption of the sanctity of life principle, is an essentially religious belief, though it is often appealed to outside any specific religious context. However, those who rely on it as an explicitly religious principle support their belief in life's sanctity by appealing to what they assert as fact: that life is the gift of God; and not only has God given life to human beings, but He in some sense still owns it, so that He alone is entitled to take it away. This is an odd and perhaps uniquely theological concept of a gift. In human terms, to give something to someone is to relinquish all rights over it, and the recipient may decide for him- or herself what to do with the thing given. Perhaps human beings might be better thought of as holding their lives in trust, or on permanent loan.

Not all religions have always regarded human life as sacred: some have required human sacrifice, many have condoned capital punishment, or burning at the stake. Nevertheless, when the Office of the Chief Rabbi presented written evidence to the House of Lords Select Committee on Lord Joffe's Assisted Dying for the Terminally Ill Bill, the submission started with the following statement:

'Jewish tradition places at its centre the sanctity of life, viewing life as a precious gift from God, not something we can dispose of at will. Indeed the value of human life is absolute and not relative to factors such as age or health … Therefore Judaism regards the value of human life as non-negotiable and insists that it cannot be compromised.' (House of Lords Select Committee on the Assisted Dying for the Terminally Ill Bill, Volume 2, p. 491)

And another Rabbi is quoted as saying:

'Any positive act designed to hasten the death of the patient is equated with murder in Jewish law, even if the death is hastened only by moments. No matter how laudable the motives of a person performing an act of mercy-killing may be, his deed constitutes an act of homicide.' (*Ibid.*)

The Church of England House of Bishops together with the Catholic Bishops' Conference were equally determined in their opposition to the Bill, and stated that their arguments grew 'out of our belief that God Himself has given to humankind the gift of life. As such, it is to be revered and cherished' (*ibid.*, p. 488). It is clear, then, that many of those who are professionally religious start from a belief that human life is sacred, that it is to be protected at all costs, and never deliberately brought to an end. Yet not all of these people are pacifists; most would probably defend the right of the armed forces to kill the enemy, however reluctantly. Most would agree with the legal plea of self-defence in a murder trial. Most would, in fact, want to distinguish the severity of the crime involved in the murder by a husband of his suffering wife, at her request, and that of a cold-blooded murderer who killed for gain or for pleasure. Some would even defend the use of the death penalty in certain circumstances. Yet it is difficult to understand how there can be exceptions to the sanctity of human life. If it is truly sacred, then nothing could justify deliberately bringing it to an end, whether by killing oneself or another, whatever the circumstances.

Moreover, few of those who defend the principle would actually advocate keeping a very severely disabled premature baby alive in an incubator, when its prospects of a tolerable life are minimal. A paediatrician who specialises in newborn babies must often be faced with the question whether or not it is right even to attempt to 'revere and cherish' this particular flicker of life, when the future prospects for the baby, if it survives for a few months or even years, are so bleak, and so full of suffering. In this kind of case, the question whether life itself is 'sacred' must frequently arise, and more so now than ever before, when it is technically possible for babies to survive after as little as 22 weeks of gestation, but when it is more than ever clear that such babies, if they live, are likely to suffer extreme disabilities. In July 2006, a working party of the Nuffield Council of Bioethics published a report (*Critical Care Decisions in Foetal and Neonatal Medicine:*

Ethical Issues, Nuffield Council of Bioethics 2006) in which it recommended that in certain circumstances newborn babies should not be kept alive artificially, but should be given 'comfort care only' until they died.

The moral difference between killing the baby and allowing it to die more slowly is hard to make out in such a case. Indeed the Working Party contemplated the possibility that the baby, once it has been consigned to certain death, should be given a lethal injection. This was turned down by a majority, apparently because the baby could not ask for it. But it was fairly clear that most thought that if the baby was in terrible pain that could not be alleviated, its death would be discreetly hastened, in the name of 'comfort'. Of course in such cases there is no direct conflict between the principle of autonomy and that of the sanctity of life, since a 22-week neonate cannot exercise autonomy; but the parents of the baby might demand treatment for it that the paediatrician thought futile or too burdensome, or indeed unjust towards other needy babies who could take this baby's place in intensive care. Part of the skill of the doctor in such a situation will be to discuss the prognosis so sympathetically yet realistically with the parents that it becomes unclear in the end whose decision it actually is that the baby should not live. But the sanctity of life is not likely to be the main issue at stake; it will be the fate of this particular precarious and much-loved human being.

At any rate, the Church of England, through its spokesman, endorsed the findings of the Nuffield Report when it came out, and made no mention of the sanctity of life. This strongly suggests that sanctity, in the absolute sense that the word requires, is not really what is relied on by those who oppose any change in the law about assisted dying, though they use the absolutist rhetoric. What most people, even those who give religious significance to 'sanctity', really mean is that human life is enormously valuable, and that causing death must never be lightly undertaken. And with this, few would quarrel. But it does not entail that there could never be circumstances in which other values had even higher priority, such as, for example, the sanctioning – however reluctantly – of the death of soldiers in defence of their country.

However this may be, I think that one needs to question the determinative assumption of the authors of the House of Lords Select Committee report, namely that the dispute about assisted dying arises from a conflict of two principles, the principle of autonomy and that of the sanctity of life. I do not believe that the nature of the dispute is best couched in terms of principles alone, though it is easy, when discussing the matter in abstract and general terms, to assume that it is. Many people who want the law to be so changed that assisted dying is occasionally permitted, start from their own particular and agonising experience of witnessing the painful death of a relative who begs to be allowed or helped to die. Neither these relatives nor the person who is dying rely on an abstract principle of autonomy. After all, most people, however strongly they hold that patients should decide on their own treatment or that they should be entitled to do what they like with their own lives, still recognise that autonomy must, as we have seen, have limits. We have no right to do exactly as we please in all circumstances, and most people recognise that the whole question is where the limits should be placed But that is not the consideration that most moves them in the situation they find themselves in. They can argue the principle in the seminar room or the debating chamber, but at the bedside it is the particular – the existing, experienced suffering – that makes them argue that the law should be changed. It is compassion, not any theory of rights, that is their motive force.

Again, if we consider the patients, whether at the very end of life, or faced with a long period of increasing pain and helplessness, the desire to bring this life to an end is seldom predominantly a matter of justice, of their supposed right to make decisions for themselves, though they may in their turn have recourse to the rhetoric of principle and rights, and may feel strongly about them. But, very often, it is the horror of total dependence on others and the loss of the privacy and self-reliance to which they have been accustomed (to say nothing of the pleasures) that makes their suffering unbearable to them. And even if they expect that as they approach death they may be mentally incapable either of taking responsibility for their own lives or even realising the full extent of their own decline, they still cannot bear the idea of getting to that stage, when they will be like a baby, looked after in every aspect of their daily life. This is the horror in prospect, even if they may know that they will not experience it as such when it comes to the time. To be reduced to this infantile condition is, as is often said, to be stripped of all dignity, in other people's eyes as well as their own, as they look ahead.

I suggest therefore that the belief that it would be morally right to allow assisted dying in some cases, and for those who truly want it for themselves, is a matter not so much of pure principle as of what in the eighteenth century was referred to as sentiment. The great difficulty faced by those who argue for a change in the law is how to draft a bill that does justice to the strong moral imperative that some people may recognise, when they cannot any longer resist the pleas of the suffering patient to be helped to die, yet a bill that will not become a licence to kill. In other words, how can one introduce compassion into the law?

This difficulty was fully understood by some of the witnesses who gave oral evidence to the House of Lords Select Committee. I quote from the Reverend Professor Robin Gill, who spoke as the representative of the Archbishop of Canterbury (*op. cit.*, p. 493). He said,

'For us as religious people compassion is directly related to our belief that God is a God of compassion and requires us to be compassionate in response to others ... I made a submission myself for Diane Pretty. I did it entirely on compassionate grounds I thought that her case represented a very very strong case indeed for voluntary euthanasia, and if it was simply a case of her and no one else ... I believe that this was as strong a case as you get and on compassionate grounds one should certainly reach out for it.'

However, as became clear as his evidence went on, he was not persuaded that the law on assisted suicide should be changed, but rather that society should accept the status quo, in which people who acted out of compassion to help their relatives to die should simply not be pursued through the courts. When challenged by a member of the committee, Baroness Hayman (later to be the first Lord Speaker of the House of Lords), to answer the question whether he was arguing for an *ex post facto* decriminalisation of assisted dying in very hard cases, and whether this was fair on the person who needed the compassionate assistance, who had to weigh up the risk of a criminal charge against the doctor or relative who gave this assistance, he, rather helplessly replied: 'What I think I am doing ... is trying to balance individual good and the common good. I think that lies at the heart of some of the most difficult quandaries in medical ethics' (*ibid.*, p. 498). He is right; but in saying this he, though a man of God, is entirely abandoning the argument from the sanctity of life. For he speaks of the assisted death on compassionate grounds of, for example, Diane Pretty, as an 'individual good' that may have to be sacrificed to the common good: that which is assumed to be the purpose of the present laws of homicide and assisted suicide.

It was, in any case, noticeable in the House of Lords that, in the debates about assisted dying, even those who started by relying on an *a priori* or theological argument that human life is sacred soon moved to reinforce this by empirical arguments about the consequences that would follow a change in the law; arguments that would have been unnecessary for them, if they had felt that the theological argument was unanswerable. It is true that it was taken for granted that the Bishops' Bench would oppose Lord Joffe's bills on grounds of faith. In a later debate on a different topic, the Bishop of Worcester recalled the 'phalanx of Bishops' who confronted Lord Joffe when he introduced his bills and said: 'This was a mark of a situation in which we have not come to a common mind and where a sense of mutual threat arises between faith and non-faith.'

Yet, as a matter of fact, one of the few speakers in the Second Reading debate on Lord Joffe's last Bill who explicitly based her argument entirely on her religious faith spoke in favour of the Bill, or at least strongly in favour of allowing it a Second Reading. This was Baroness Richardson of Calow, a committed Christian and a Minister in the Methodist Church. She said:

'There is no doubt that this Bill has shocked the religious communities. It has shocked us because we have had to look at ourselves in a new light. It has undermined the security that some have felt that God is in control of life and death and that therefore our responsibility has to be simply to assist Him in what is the best we can arrange; the most comfort, the deepest love, and the highest level of care. Into the hands of men and women has now been put a great responsibility over life and death, and it is no longer safe to talk about "natural life" as though we have defined it. If we have in our hands the means by which a person can end their suffering we must ask: What are the moral judgments we must make to withhold that?' (*Hansard* HL, 12 May 2006, cols 1244–1245).

There were others too who spoke of seeing no contradiction between allowing assisted dying and Christian theology.

Very few people appeared to notice that there was any difference between absolutist arguments based on faith rather than fact, and empirical arguments which require supporting evidence. An exception to this was the Labour peer, the late Lord Carter, who declared his opposition to the Bill in these words:

'The sanctity of life argument – perhaps I may call it that – is not my reason for opposing this legislation. As legislators, our religious beliefs are bound to inform our deliberations, but our overriding concern and responsibility should be to consider the best interests of society as a whole, that is for those with religious beliefs and those without.' (*Ibid.*)

He then went on to argue against the Bill on the grounds of its supposed adverse consequences for society. Similarly, Lord Winston said:

'I am an orthodox Jew and I believe in the basic principle of *pikuach nefesh*, which is essentially the principle of the sanctity of human life. But we live in a pluralistic society and it is very important that when we make legislation and talk about these issues, while our personal background may influence and illuminate our opinion, it must be very important and clear to us that we do not expect our opinion necessarily to dominate those of other people. So I will set aside completely my religious views and speak from a purely secular point of view.' (*Ibid.*)

He then, like Lord Carter, went on to oppose the bill, on broadly consequentialist grounds. It is open to question whether it is possible for a truly religious person to speak from a wholly secular point of view; this is what makes the discussion of the relation between religion and the law so difficult. But this will be further discussed in the next chapter.

The consequentialist arguments against assisted dying can be divided into three kinds: those broadly speaking arising from the fear that any permissive law will be abused, those derived from a consideration of the proper duty of doctors and nurses, and those special arguments put forward by people involved in palliative care. These empirical arguments are sometimes classed together as Slippery Slope or Foot-in-the door arguments, and I have so classed them myself (see *Easeful Death*, chapter 7), but I think that to do so probably obscures significant differences between them, and between the people who propound them, though it is plainly possible for the same person to rely on arguments from more than one category.

The first and most formidable set of arguments is that of those people, predominantly lawyers, who believe that it would be impossible to draft a law in which voluntary euthanasia or assisted suicide was so hedged about by conditions and safeguards that it could not be abused. As with all the arguments we are now considering, since there is no such law at present on the statute book in the UK, accounts of the consequences that would follow if such a law were introduced, are bound to be speculative, though these consequences are often said to be 'inevitable'. A colourful Australian, Chris Wake, is quoted as opposing the short-lived law in the Northern Territory that permitted voluntary euthanasia (overturned by Federal Government after nine months) in these words:

'The rationale on which I oppose this bill has nothing to do with religion. The argument needs fighting on earth here and now, not in heaven hereafter ... It's the socio-economic aspects of euthanasia being applied in Australia which frightens me to death, because I think, in fact I KNOW it would be misused. And I haven't seen anything anywhere in the world that comes within a coo-ee of ensuring that abuse would not occur.' (Quoted in Miriam Cosic, *The Right to Die: An Examination of the Euthanasia Debate*, New Holland 2003, p. 164)

Lord Joffe's bills all contained conditions that had to be satisfied if assistance to die was to be permitted: for example, that two doctors must certify that the patient was mentally competent; that the patient must sign a document stating their wish to die; that they must have alternatives explained to them; that they might change their mind at any time during the period that must elapse between their formal request and their death taking place. But still the safeguards were not enough for the lawyers. They were, in the words of the Liberal Democrat peer and lawyer, Lord Carlile of Beriew, 'paper-thin'.

Though in the nature of the case there can be no evidence of abuse of the law in this country, those opposed to liberalisation have frequently cited evidence, by analogy, from what they see as the abuse of the Abortion Law, through gradual relaxation of the criteria for permitting abortion for social reasons. It is not clear, however, that this is a sound analogy. There are far more people who suffer unwanted pregnancies than there are people who want to die when they are terminally ill. At first sight, a stronger source of evidence might be any known abuse of the law in those countries where either euthanasia or assisted suicide is lawful, the Netherlands, Belgium, and the states of Oregon and Washington in the USA (in Switzerland the situation is different: assisted death is not generally lawful, but only to members of the special institution, Dignitas). However, the evidence from other legislatures is difficult to assess. Those opposed to liberalisation tend to produce figures to show that widespread abuse of the law exists; those in favour find the opposite. All depends on what questions are asked.

The real conviction that there would be abuse stems not so much from evidence or analogy as from certain beliefs about human nature. First, and most generally, it is argued that the consequence of allowing assisted death, however much hedged about with safeguards, will be to lift a taboo, which will entail that death begins to seem like a genuine option among others, to be considered in the treatment of someone who is terminally ill, or suffering from an incurable condition. Of course it already is a genuine option, in the case, for instance, of someone in a permanent vegetative state, who may be allowed to die by the withholding of nutrition and hydration, but to permit this involves the judgement of a court in each individual case. But, it is argued, if this permission is even partially generalised and written into a statute, so that there are prescribed cases where a person may choose to die at another's hands, then society will become used to the idea of killing and there will be no trust left. In 1965, in a different context, Lord Devlin wrote:

'A murderer who acts only upon the consent and maybe the request of his victim, is no menace to others, but he does threaten one of the great moral principles upon which society is based, that is the sanctity of human life. There is only one explanation for what has hitherto been accepted as the basis for the criminal law, and that is that there are certain moral principles which society is required to observe and the breach of them is an offence not merely against the person who is injured but against society as a whole.' (Patrick Devlin, *The Enforcement of Morals*, Oxford University Press 1965, p. 6)

Here the principle of the sanctity of life has no necessarily religious connotation. It was taken by Lord Devlin to be a moral and a legal fact that the principle is fundamental to society, and it is used in an empirical argument, relying on the supposed consequences of allowing it to be weakened. The consequence of its breach is the ultimate destruction of society. Killing is indeed taboo, and if the law were changed, the psychological attitude towards murder would change too.

There is another belief about human nature that underlies predictions of harm to society from a liberalisation of the law. It is widely held that it is always rational to want to live, whatever the quality of life; and that therefore those who express a wish that they might die are either mentally deranged, or do not really mean what they say. They have had pressure put on them by their relatives to claim to want to die when their real will is to live. There are variants of this belief. Some think that children will begin plotting the death of their parent, let us say, as soon as the law is changed, so that they may inherit money, or be relieved of the trouble and expense (of both resources and time) that is taken looking after the old things, and will actually suggest death as a preferable and now lawful option. Others may not think these children will be so crude and grasping, but nevertheless believe that parents will come to think that, now that they may lawfully seek help to do so, they have a duty to end their lives for the sake of their children, or whoever is caring for them. The point was made very clearly in the debate on Lord Joffe's last Bill, when it was denied a Second Reading (*Hansard* HL, Friday, 12 May 2006, col. 1211). Lord Tombs in a short speech said this:

'Terminally ill people are vulnerable people, afraid and apprehensive about approaching death and the manner of its arrival. They are very sensitive to suggestion, and there is no shortage of potential coercive influences ... Acceptance by the law of the deliberate termination of life, albeit at the patient's request, could create an ambience in which the patient felt pressured to comply. The feeling of being a burden on others is familiar to many elderly and disabled people and it would be all too easy for a right to opt for a deliberate death to become a duty to do so for the sake of others. The exception would then become normal irrespective of the real wishes and welfare of the patient.'

I personally think that the desire not to be a burden is something that should in most cases be treated as genuine and sincere, not written of as pretended. This kind of altruism is reasonable, even laudable as a motive, and should be respected. It is certainly in general considered admirable that parents should value the well-being of their children as highly as their own. But altruism in death does not seem to be equally admired, and would be taken by many as a sign either of undue pressure or of insanity. In any case, whether the so-called coercive influences are overt or hidden, the person who seeks death is labelled by the objectors as 'vulnerable', and it is deemed even worse to kill the vulnerable than those who might put up a fight.

The word 'vulnerable' has become a powerful rhetorical tool, in recent years. A society is said to be judged civilised or the reverse according to how well it looks after the vulnerable, which include children, the sick, the old and the disabled. The parable of the Good Samaritan, encapsulating as it does the virtue of compassion, illustrates the Christian tradition of care for the vulnerable, and it is a story that is readily intelligible to non-Christians too. Yet there may, for the old and the sick at least, be something oppressive about repeatedly being referred to as vulnerable. It may imply a degree of helplessness that they would not feel if it were not imposed on them. It suggests incompetence to make decisions, an incapability of assigning proper values to things and a consequent subjection to other people's value-system. There is a kind of arrogance in the assumption that the aged or the sick are to be classed with children and the insane, unable to form their own judgements or know what they really want. The 'vulnerable' are subject to influence, sometimes even bullying by others stronger than they; it is the strong who decide that they have got to live when they would honestly prefer to die, and this in the name of a compassionate society. When the bishops switch from their impregnable argument that God is the giver of the sacred gift of life (impregnable in the sense that it is theological and thus not supported by evidence or capable of proof), it is to the vulnerability of the terminally ill or otherwise suffering that they turn. Thus, in the letter from the Church of England House of Bishops and the Catholic Bishops' Conference of England and Wales to the House of Lords Select Committee from which I have already quoted (pp. 488–489), we find the following:

'The arguments presented in this submission grow out of our belief that God himself has given to humankind the gift of life ... All human beings are to be valued irrespective of age, sex, race, religion, social status or their potential for achievement. Those who become vulnerable through illness or disability deserve special care and protection. Adherence to this principle provides a fundamental test as to what constitutes a civilised society. The whole of humankind is the recipient of God's gift of life. Life is to be received with gratitude and used responsibly. Human beings each have their own distinct identities, but these are formed by and take their place within complex networks of relationships. All decisions about individual lives bear upon others with whom we live in community. For this reason, the law relating to euthanasia is not simply concerned with private morality ... This is one of the issues, relatively few in number but of fundamental importance, in which justice calls for a limit to moral or ethical pluralism. A positive choice has to be made by society in favour of protecting its vulnerable members, even if this means limiting the freedom of others to determine their end.'

But suppose the 'vulnerable members' do not want the protection of society? Suppose those 'others' who are to be sacrificed, their freedom limited, are the very 'vulnerable members' themselves? There may seem something patronising and perverse about insisting that 'the vulnerable' must be protected even against their will, forced to live because they are too ignorant or too carefully supervised or simply too weak to be able to take their own lives.

The group of arguments against liberalising the law that turn on the fear of abuse, and especially the abuse of the vulnerable, reaches its most intense point in the arguments of what has come to be called the disabled lobby. They disregard altogether the central condition of any liberalising legislation, that the patient's death must be voluntary. They simply suggest that the step from a death that has been requested to one that has not is negligible, and will quite certainly be taken. For they argue that others, who are not disabled, regard the life of someone with a severe disability as not worth living, and therefore dispensable, overlooking the fact that a liberalised law would be concerned to help only those who, for whatever reason, had ceased to value their own continued life What other people think of the quality of the life of a disabled person has no relevance. As Lady Hale, one of the Law Lords who judged Debbie Purdey's case, put it: 'It is not for society to tell people what to value about their own lives' (quoted in Tony Delamothe, 'The Assisted Dying Debate has been Hijacked', *British Medical Journal* 339 (2009), p. 3446). And it is not the disabled alone who use this argument. Those who speak from a specifically Christian or other religious point of view are inclined to rely on it as well, because of the close historic link between religion and charity to the 'vulnerable'. Thus the Archbishop of Canterbury, who opposed Lord Joffe's Bill in 2006, wrote an article in the *British Medical Journal* in which he discerned in the Bill a 'message' that 'certain kinds of life are not worth living' (*British Medical Journal* 337 (2006), p. 1169). Laws are not made to send out messages, but to make things better; but, that apart, it is genuinely confusing to oppose assisted dying legislation while overlooking the safeguards there would have to be to ensure that the patient and the patient alone had concluded that his or her life is no longer worth living.

I come now to a second group of consequentialist or empirical arguments against liberalisation, used primarily, though not exclusively, by the medical and nursing professions, and relying on the supposed effects of a change in the law. These can be treated more briefly. It must be remembered that, despite the move against paternalism and towards patient autonomy, doctors remain in a position of strength in the debate over assisted dying. Almost nobody supposes that doctors and nurses will be left out of the actual prescribing or administering of fatal doses if assisted death is ever made lawful. Their hostility to a change in the law could therefore be decisive. It is far from clear how widespread such hostility is. The Royal College of Nursing has now advised its members that they may discuss assisted dying with their patients; and there is certainly a considerable number of doctors who are in favour of the change. But the orthodox line remains: doctors and nurses exist to preserve and protect lives, not to bring them to an end. Though they may not lawfully treat patients against their will, if they refuse treatment it is the medical staff's duty to care for them and alleviate their symptoms as far as possible, to keep them alive until their life draws to its natural end and nature takes its course. If at this stage of someone's life the doctor increases the dose of painkillers and the patient dies, the doctor has recourse to the argument from double effect: the intention was not to kill the patient but to ease their pain. Death was an unwanted side-effect for which the doctor cannot be held responsible. (In fact the argument from double effect, always intensely suspect and casuistical relying as it does on an implausible cut-off point for responsibility, is now less useful to doctors than hitherto. For there are new drugs for alleviating pain that do not have a potentially lethal effect.) But in any case, doctors do deliberately and knowingly cause the death of their patients, especially in hospital, when they may decide that no attempt should be made to resuscitate a patient if he or she suffers heart failure, or when they decide that further treatment would be futile or too burdensome to be continued. They feel no guilt in taking such decisions, since they rely on a distinction between killing someone (active intervention) and allowing someone to die. This distinction seems to me to have little moral foundation; in each case a decision has been taken that a life shall be brought to an end. Yet the verb 'to kill' has a powerful negative connotation, and if doctors can avoid using it, they will be saved from feelings of responsibility. Doctors have been known to say that they *cannot* kill people: they are hard-wired to do them good, not harm. This must surely be an exaggeration (see Warnock and Macdonald, *op. cit.*, pp. 93–94).

The second part of the medical argument is that not only doctors but also their patients rely on the assumption that the doctor's role is to cure and not to kill, and that therefore, if it were known that assisted death were an option, the trust between doctor and patient would be eroded. It has to be said that, since most people die in hospital where they do not know their doctors, and since most patients, if they are very old or very ill, understand that, with the health service having limited resources, they cannot expect unlimited free treatment, the trust between patients and doctors has already been pretty fatally eroded. But where terminally ill patients are in the hands of a doctor whom they know and trust, what they want and expect the doctor to do in many cases is not to cure them, not even to keep them alive, but to make their dying bearable.

Finally, there is a sub-group of medical arguments of a specialist nature deployed by those who are involved in palliative care.

Ideally, palliative care – that is, care of terminally ill patients directed towards the relief of symptoms, the management of pain, and psychological support for those who know they are dying, and for their families – should be available to everyone. It should simply be part of medical treatment, and in many countries, including the Netherlands where assisted dying is lawful, palliative medicine was for long not counted as a special branch of medicine, though this has recently changed. Here, palliative medicine is a specialism, partly because of its history. It used to be practised only in designated nursing homes or hospices, and the Hospice movement was founded as a private charity to provide beds for terminal cancer patients, where they could be cared for by specialists in pain relief, and by people experienced in offering comfort for the dying of a specifically Christian character. At first the movement was funded entirely by donation, and it is still largely reliant on donations and legacies. Though it was not essential that a patient be a Christian to get a hospice bed, the consolations of the Christian religion were almost a part of the treatment. Now its scope has widened; and palliative care is provided at home as well as in hospices, and great advances have been made in the understanding and management of pain. Moreover, patients other than cancer sufferers are increasingly treated at the end of their lives. But provision is still limited, some parts of the country being far worse off than others, and NHS support is extremely variable. There is also a need for further research, for example into pain management, and the specialists in the field have a real and understandable fear that if voluntary assisted dying became lawful, funding for research would dry up. If it were generally believed that hospices might offer voluntary death as well as care and comfort to their patients, charitable funding, especially that from specifically religious sources, might also dwindle. There are specialists who admit that palliative care, even in its modern more comprehensive and

CHAPTER THREE

The Law and Moral Values

We have seen in the last two chapters that in those parliamentary legislative debates that have been most obviously concerned with moral issues, matters of life and death, there is a tangle of morality and religion, of the empirical and the *a priori*, matters of value and matters of faith, as well as speculation about the future. Somewhere in this tangle people find the convictions upon which they base their judgement and determine their vote. And it is not in the least surprising that the interface between morals and religion is obscure. The teaching of religion and that of morals – what it is one's duty to believe and what it is one's duty to do and to avoid – has, through the ages, gone hand in hand. Indeed it has been the same teaching, whether in school or in church, synagogue or mosque. It is only in fairly recent times that education has been deliberately secularised, even in the numerous schools founded by the Church of England, while at the same time church attendance (and presumably attendance at Sunday School) has steeply declined.

In most schools the teaching of religion and that of morality have been gradually prised apart. Morality, if taught at all, is taught separately under the guise of Social and Personal Development, or Citizenship, or even Sex Education, while religion in most schools is something to be taught from the outside, as a kind of anthropology, or perhaps philosophy. Teachers have become fearful of being thought to indoctrinate, and of breaching the code of total tolerance in a 'multifaith' and 'multicultural' society. Pluralism, and an equal respect for all faiths, is the only value attached to religious teaching. Though church schools may prefer to employ teachers who are members of the Church, and though they are still legally permitted to do so, they may often have difficulty in finding candidates. So, both in church and secular schools, religious education has greatly diminished, becoming, in secondary schools, an optional examinable subject like history or geography. Moreover, because of the close relation hitherto existing between religion and morality, there is a widespread assumption that, along with a multiplicity of faiths, there must be a multiplicity of morals, so universal respect and tolerance must be extended to questions of morality as well as of faith, different moralities being part and parcel of different cultures. At all costs, no one must be offended. It is perhaps not so much in the classroom curriculum as in the general policy of the school (such as, for example 'zero tolerance' of bullying) that one can find definite and unequivocal moral principles being taught.

The exception to the trend towards equality of esteem for all religions and of respect for all 'people of Faith', whatever it is that they believe in, has been in Roman Catholic, Jewish and above all in Muslim schools, where there is still held not only to be one true faith, but also the old and inextricable bond between religion and morality. The crucial difference between these religions and the Church of England and nonconformist churches lies in a difference in the authority claimed by the leaders of the faiths, and the submission to that authority by its followers. For people educated in such Faith schools, where orthodoxy is at least strongly encouraged, it is natural to take for granted the link between faith and morality, and, in later life, such people often express moral opinions learned in childhood and adolescence without feeling the need explicitly to mention their religious connections.

There is another very obvious explanation for the fact that few people, in Parliament at least, openly state that their opposition to liberalising 'moral' legislation derives from religious belief. Faith is traditionally contrasted with reason; and no one engaged in debate wishes to appear unreasonable. By definition, what is a matter of faith cannot be proved or disproved. Argument is therefore an inappropriate tool with which to confront it. So if argument is to be engaged in, as it must, in the course of the passage of a Bill through Parliament, of necessity those who rely on faith must do their best to downplay that fact, or at least show that they have reason on their side as well.

That it has been difficult to distinguish between moral and religious arguments over the essentially moral issues I have so far considered does not entail that there is really no difference between them, or that the difference is not significant. I shall later try to show that one set of arguments – that based on moral considerations – has logical priority over those based on faith, religion itself being, in part, an expression of pre-existing moral beliefs. However, for the time being I intend to set on one side the distinction between the moral and the religious, in order to examine, albeit superficially, the relation between morality and the law, regardless of where that morality may be held to originate, and whether or not moral goodness is thought to be obedience to God's laws as revealed to His people.

It is necessary here to consider the history of English jurisprudence. For Jeremy Bentham (1748–1832) the relation between morality and law held no problems. Both law and morality stemmed from the same source, namely the Principle of Utility. According to this principle, whatever individual or corporate actions, or whatever laws, tend to result in the greatest happiness of the greatest number are good; whatever have the opposite tendency are bad. This is the meaning of 'good' and 'bad'. Happiness is a state where pleasure is greater than pain. The difference between a law and a moral principle was, on this theory, that a law was a command issued by a sovereign power by due process, and that there were sanctions attached to its breach, whereas a moral principle was simply generally adopted, on the ground that it was conducive to the Greatest Happiness principle. (That the Command theory of law, like the Imperative theory of morality, is inadequate need not here concern us.)

Thus both a moral principle and a law could be judged at the same tribunal, that of utility, or the greatest happiness of the greatest number. And in this belief, Bentham devoted himself to his life-work, the codification and rationalisation of laws, not merely of his own country but of others, since the principle of utility was universally valid. He thought that he would be able, by using this criterion, to throw out those laws whose effect was bad, retaining only those whose effect was good. He believed that it was possible to measure both the quantity and the intensity of pleasures and pains, and that by using these measurements, he could assess the overall sum of pleasure that any law or moral principle would tend to produce.

Accordingly, in 1789 he published a work entitled *An Introduction to the Principles of Morals and Legislation*, in which he set out what he called a calculus of pleasures and pains (the felicific calculus) for the purpose of this measurement. It did not make any difference whose pleasures or pains were considered. The principle of utility considered the pleasures and pains of the whole of society indifferently; and the reason for the duty to obey the law (apart from the fear of sanctions) as well as for adhering to a moral principle, was that, as each person was a part of the great democratic public for whose happiness the laws or principles should work, obedience was in everyone's interest.

Bentham thus rejected the idea that there was such a thing as a higher law, whether Natural, Moral or Divine, standing above actual laws, and in accordance with the dictates of which the laws of a particular society were made. The principle of utility was not itself such a law. It was simply a matter of fact that it is according to utility that people count things good or bad. He also rejected the idea, expounded by Hobbes among other political theorists, that obedience to the law was cemented by an original contract, under the terms of which people had agreed to obey the laws in exchange for the benefits of society. If there were such Natural Laws, or if there had been such a binding Original Contract, it would entail that morality somehow preceded law. For the doctrine of Natural Law, which is also Moral Law, assumed that actual, positive laws derived their validity from their being as far as possible reflections of Natural Law. The Original Contract assumed that it made sense to speak of contracts and contractual obligations before society existed. Both doctrines (of which I am concerned only with the first) thus presume that morality takes precedence over law and is both its origin and its justification.

This Bentham denied. Though it was, for him, of the greatest importance to distinguish between law and morality, both were equally justified by the principle of utility, and by that alone. In that sense they were on a level. He scathingly attacked the concepts of both Natural Law and the Original Contract in his first published work, 'A Fragment on Government' (published anonymously in 1776). This was an onslaught on Sir William Blackstone's influential *Commentary on the Laws of England* where he had expounded both doctrines.

In Bentham's jurisprudence, therefore, morality and legislation, though distinct, were completely interlocked as to their origins and their purpose, neither having priority, logical or temporal, over the other. But scrutiny of the effects of a law either before it was enacted or when it was already on the statute book was always possible, and was indeed a democratic duty. Bentham's advice to those living under the laws of any state was 'to obey punctually; to censure freely' ('A Fragment on Government', in *Works* 230, Preface, para. 16). The criticism could be made only according to the Greatest Happiness principle, by which alone the goodness or the badness of anything whatever, including a law, could be judged.

Yet the notion that morality is somehow superior to the law and flows from a different source has always been attractive. In some cases, it is true, it might be possible to show, on strictly utilitarian principles, as Bentham hoped to do, that the existence of a law, or the fixed sentence that it carried, had adverse consequences for society as a whole, causing more pain than pleasure, or harm than good. In such a case a Utilitarian would have to agree that the law was defective, according to the principle of utility, and this would be a victory of the moral over the legal application of the principle. When the penalty for sheep-stealing was hanging, for instance, it could have been argued that the outcome was that there would be thefts of more valuable animals ('As well be hung for a sheep as a lamb'), and that the sentence was so grossly disproportionate anyway that few felons would be convicted. And if there is a law on the statute book that is never enforced, or is incapable of enforcement, that in itself can be seen to be harmful to society, liable to bring the law as a whole into contempt. In such cases, Utilitarianism can by itself justify the removal of the law from the statute book.

It is worth remarking, at this point, that whether or not one is a strict Benthamite, it cannot be denied that the principle of utility, at least in some refined form, must play a major part in legislation; for legislators must ask, of any proposed law, will the consequences of enacting it bring more benefit to society than harm, more good than ill; in Bentham's terminology, more pleasure than pain? And we have seen in the two preceding chapters how frequently this question is formulated by parliamentarians, as they contemplate the slippery slope down which society will supposedly slide if a particular piece of legislation is agreed to. It is also worth repeating that frequently the term 'utilitarian' is used not to designate Bentham's Greatest Happiness principle, but, confusingly, to refer derogatively to a system of values that elevates the immediately profitable or the materialistic over more long-term or morally respectable outcomes. I sometimes wish that there could be an embargo on the use of the term, except in strictly historical contexts.

However that may be, there can be no doubt that the principle of utility or the Greatest Happiness principle, as expounded by Bentham, is inadequate to determine all questions of morality. Most people recognise that there may be a conflict between law and morality that cannot be settled by seeing whether the effect of the law causes more pleasure than pain (even if finding this out were as simple as Bentham believed). For example, a Benthamite calculus of pleasure and pain might show that in some circumstances it would be right to lock up someone whom you alone knew to be innocent of a crime, if society thought him guilty and would get satisfaction and a sense of security from his imprisonment. A Benthamite might try to prove that Utilitarianism could not have such consequences as these, by arguing that injustice is intrinsically wrong, even if it is unrecognised, and would therefore in the long term be harmful to society. But if he argued thus he would have ceased to be a strict Utilitarian, and would have embarked on a different system of morality, one that not only may be in conflict with positive law, but must be defended on different grounds from those of the Greatest Happiness principle, grounds that must refer to justice and fairness. The conflict in such a case is between what is right and what is expedient, a kind of conflict that Utilitarianism finds it difficult to recognise or to explain.

And many politicians find the same difficulty today. The recent dispute in Parliament over the length of time that someone suspected of terrorist activities might be kept in custody before being charged is an example of such a conflict. To retain a suspect for 92 days, as the legislation first proposed, was held to be morally repugnant, because unjust, however much many readers of the *Daily Mail* might rejoice, and however deep and widespread their satisfaction might be, at the prospect.

Such conflicts as these have been known from ancient times, and are often described, in terms that Blackstone would have recognised and approved, by reference to a higher law, natural or divine. So Sophocles represented Antigone, in his play of that name, as defying the Theban tyrant, Kreon, who had prohibited her by law from burying her brother. In her great speech to Kreon, she invokes a higher law than any mere earthly law, under which she has not only a right to show respect to her dead brother, but a positive duty to do so. She is claiming both her right and her obligation to scatter earth on his grave, and both are accorded her by the higher law.

The logical connection between the concept of rights and that of law can hardly be denied. If someone successfully claims a right, they must do so on the basis of a law that confers the right on them. Thus, to use the language of inalienable moral rights or human rights itself suggests an appeal to a higher moral law. Ramblers, for example, can now claim the Right to Roam under the Countryside Act (2005), yet many of them protested, before the law was enacted, that they already had a moral right to enjoy the countryside. Parents can claim that their child has a legal right to education, however severe the child's disabilities, only since the Education Act of 1972 conferred such a right on all those children hitherto classed as ineducable. But many parents, and those campaigning for universal education, would have claimed that every child has an inalienable right to be educated, whatever education laws may say. If the connection between rights and laws is, as these examples tend to suggest, a matter of logic, then to talk about a moral or human right must entail a moral law, a law governing all human beings, which confers such rights.

Bentham certainly held that there could, logically, be no right without a law that conferred it, which at the same time imposed a duty on others not to prevent the bearer of that right from enjoying it. But by 'law' he meant a 'positive' law that had been enacted by a sovereign power, and that had a sanction annexed to it; in other words, an existing law. He thought that to speak of a right not so conferred, but conferred by Nature (or Natural Law) was 'nonsense upon stilts' (Jeremy Bentham, 'Anarchical Fallacies' 1791, in *2 Works*, p. 491 – written in response to the French Declaration of Human Rights). His scathing attack on Blackstone was published only a few months before the American Declaration of Independence was signed, which famously invoked the doctrine that all men are born equal and are possessed of natural and inalienable rights. Governments, according to this doctrine, are set up to secure these rights, and they acquire their just powers by the consent of those whom they govern. Bentham would have none of this. By denouncing Blackstone's concept of Natural Law as meaningless, he was, as he put it, tearing 'the mask of mystery' from the face of jurisprudence. The mysteriousness, the obfuscation, was caused, he thought, by the pretence that one could meaningfully talk of a moral law founded on anything but the principle of utility. Words such as 'ought' made sense only if they were interpreted as referring to what would produce more pleasure than pain. When otherwise interpreted they were meaningless. Thus both law and morality were derived from the principle of utility, since both generated concepts such as 'duty', or what 'ought' to be done. But it was essential to distinguish law as it exists, placed by due process on the statute book, and with sanctions attached, from law as it ought to exist, judged by the standard of utility. Otherwise it would be impossible to criticise existing laws; but also it would be possible to defend disregarding them, in the name of a higher law. A belief in Natural Law was therefore not only nonsensical, but dangerous nonsense.

Bentham maintained that there is only one kind of law, and that is positive law. His complaint against Blackstone was that by insisting on another law lying behind the actual law of a land he obscured the essential separation of law from morals. There are good positive laws and bad positive laws; that is, laws conducive to utility or the reverse. The principle of utility alone can distinguish good from bad, but the principle of utility is, as I have said, not itself a law. It has never been enacted; it simply provides the meaning of the words 'good' and 'bad'. There is no 'higher' law, which, according to some different and mysterious standard, could impose different imperatives or confer different rights. If, as Antigone supposed, Kreon's law was a bad law it was so because it offended against the principle of utility, and according to the same principle it should be revoked.

Bentham was a legal positivist, then, in that he held that you could not claim a right unless you could point to the law that conferred it. All you could claim was that you ought to have a right, that is, that the law ought to be so changed as to confer the right upon you. But one need not be a Benthamite Utilitarian to be a legal positivist. You could argue that you ought to have this right in the interest not of your, or anyone else's, greatest happiness, but in the interest of justice or because of your great need, where compassion would determine what ought to be the positive law. The logical connection between actual rights and positive existing law could be upheld, provided you were prepared always to make your claim in terms not of what was your right, but of the rights that justice or compassion or custom required that you should be granted. Legal positivism could then be preserved, as long as everyone who claimed a right was careful to distinguish what was an existing right from what was a right they ought to be legally granted, despite having no right to it under present law. This 'right-one-ought-to-be-granted' could, for short, be referred to as a moral right, dependent upon a moral law or principle. To adopt such a way of referring to rights would, in my opinion, add considerably to clarity in the matter of rights. It would also place morality where I believe it belongs, as having ultimate priority over the law, often, though not necessarily always, the basis on which we must judge whether a law is good or bad, whether it should remain unamended or should be repealed or amended.

However, I do not believe that such greater clarity in the discourse of rights could ever be imposed. After all, those who want to be permitted to do something to which they feel they are morally entitled, as the ramblers felt they were morally entitled to have free access to the acres of privately owned land in the UK, prefer, perhaps need, to make rhetorical use of the language of rights. To claim a right to roam where the law currently forbids you to go sounds as if you already have something the use of which you are being unjustly refused. It is as if someone refused me entry to my own house, bought with my own money, the owner of the title deeds. No one who wishes to protest about their rights would willingly forgo the borrowed certainty and righteous indignation derived from legal rights and enacted laws. Legal rights can be proved, by reference to the law, and in the courts. Moral rights depend on moral laws, or moral principles; a much more contentious and slippery matter, unless, like Bentham, you believe that the principle of utility and the felicific calculus can show definitively what is morally good or evil.

At any rate, legal positivism, with its separation of what is legal from what is moral, became an unacceptable doctrine in the second half of the twentieth century, partly no doubt because of the increasingly perceived moral inadequacy of strict Benthamite Utilitarianism, with its tendency, already noticed, towards sacrificing the individual to some common or community good, its potential disregard for justice towards individuals.

Perhaps more importantly, it came to be recognised that if there were no rights except those conferred by actual positive laws, then in regimes in which there were laws that deprived people of what seemed obviously their rights, there was no basis left from which these rights could be claimed. The law is the law: if you were a Jew in Germany in the 1930s, you could claim no actual right to your property or even your life. The existing law entitled the state to strip you of both. The Benthamite separation of law from morals thus seemed to justify the conspicuous failure of German lawyers during the Nazi era to protest at the enormity of the things they were required to do in the name of the law. The concept of inalienable human rights of which nobody should be deprived by any law began to seem more and more necessary as a basis for disputing the validity of existing laws, which were immoral by any standard of morality. These universal human rights would be distinct from legal rights, but no law could be held to be valid unless it respected them. A positive law, to be a law, must itself incorporate an element of justice, that is, of morality.

Such was the view that began to prevail in jurisprudence. And in UK legislation, the Human Rights Act (1998) now requires that whoever is introducing a Bill into either House of Parliament shall make a declaration at the beginning of each published Bill that in his view the provisions of the Bill are compatible with the European Convention of Human Rights, and the Bill as a whole can be challenged on these grounds.

It could be argued that such an element of morality has always been already present in the common law, and can be made explicit by judges in interpreting the law, as they must do, taking into account the purpose or spirit of the law, but without any explicit appeal to human rights. Thus the purpose of the law of homicide is to protect people from murder. With the coming into existence of human embryos alive as discrete individual entities in the laboratory, some people suggested that it should be left to the courts to decide whether the destruction of such embryos was covered by the law of homicide or not. And when the Committee of Inquiry into Human Fertilisation and Embryology was set up, our first task was to decide whether new legislation was necessary or not. In fact, the committee quickly agreed that the purpose of the law of homicide was to protect living human beings who had been born, adults and children, from harm at the hands of another such human being, and the question of the destruction or protection of embryos in the laboratory was not part of its purpose. Totally new legislation was here required, rather than interpretation of the old law. But there are many cases where a judge may decide that the scope of a law may be extended to cover something unforeseen by its makers, if the extension seems to accord with what the law-makers intended to effect by the law, and if, as is usually the case, one may assume that their intention was to protect people from some harm, or entitle them to some good. If ball games are prohibited in a public garden, it must be a matter for decision whether games of Frisbee are permitted. Since such games are likely to cause as much disturbance as ball games, it might be thought to be in the spirit of the original by-law, in accordance with its intentions (namely, to preserve the peace and quiet of the garden) to prohibit games played with a Frisbee as well. It is not only the words of the law that must be considered, but what the point of it was. In this spirit, in the course of a long judgment of the Court of Appeal, Lord Justice Denning wrote:

'Whenever a statute comes up for consideration it must be remembered that it is not within human powers to foresee the manifold sets of facts which may arise, and, even if it were, it is not possible to provide for them in terms free from all ambiguity ... This is where the draftsmen of Acts of Parliament have often been unfairly criticised. A judge, supposing himself to be fettered by the supposed rule that he should look to the language and nothing else laments that the draftsmen have not provided for this or that or have been guilty of some other ambiguity. It would certainly save the judges trouble if Acts of Parliament were drafted with divine prescience and perfect clarity. In the absence of it, when a defect appears a judge cannot simply fold his hands and blame the draftsman. He must set to work on the constructive task of finding the intention of Parliament, and he must do this not only from the language but also from consideration of the social conditions which gave rise to it, and the mischief which it was passed to remedy and then he must supplement it so as to give "force and life" to the intention of the legislature ... A judge should ask himself the question: if the makers of the Act had themselves come across this ruck in the texture of it, how would they have straightened it out? (Quoted in Edmund Heward, *Lord Denning: A Biography*, Barry Rose Law Publishers 2002, p. 103)

(But Lord Justice Denning, it has to be said, came up with some pretty bizarre 'straightenings out' of his own.)

All the same, in the light of our knowledge that some laws, and even some whole legal systems, cannot be assumed to be benevolent in their intentions, it has increasingly seemed necessary to incorporate within a legislature itself protection for those rights which are most basic and most necessary if human life is to be tolerable. The Human Rights Act (1998), however much Bentham would have objected to it as nonsense upon stilts, is there to show that legislators, in making laws, are bound by the dictates of justice and morality.

America, from the beginning, had a Bill of Rights. And there was the United Nations Declaration of Human Rights (1948), drawn up in the aftermath of the Nazi and other atrocities, which set out a list of the basic rights, such as would have been conferred on everyone by the Natural Law in which Blackstone (and Sophocles) believed. But it did not itself have the status of law. It was more in the nature of a treaty or convention, agreed between countries; it was passed by no due process of legislation, but agreed round a table and ratified country by country. There were, it is true, mechanisms for appeal to international courts, if a human right appeared to have been violated; and everyone understood what was meant if a country was said to have a 'bad human rights record'. Yet it seemed to many jurists in the UK that more needed to be done to protect citizens from arbitrary or unjust legislation. And so the process of drafting the Human Rights Bill began.

However, there is not and could never be, a definitive list of human rights. To claim that your rights have been infringed is to claim that you have been unjustly treated in some specific way; and there are infinitely many ways that people may feel thus aggrieved. Though precedents are gradually emerging, to which judges may look in making human rights decisions, in the end they must rely on a moral judgement to decide whether or not an infringement of human rights has occurred. They must ask themselves: ought any human being to be treated in the way this human being has been treated? Is such treatment morally tolerable? Though the answers to these questions are judicial answers, and legally binding, they are undoubtedly also questions of morals. Diane Pretty, as we saw, claimed that she had a right to die at a point in her progressive illness before her life would become intolerable to her. The International Court at Strasbourg did not uphold her claim. Whether or not someone might claim a right to die must, so they ruled, depend on the state of the positive existing law of the particular country from which he or she came. There was no universally compelling moral principle demanding that anyone in the world should be allowed this freedom to choose death. In the Netherlands, there is such a right; in the UK there is not. Inalienable human rights are not involved. Such was the decision of the court. Another court at another time might have ruled differently.

If the foregoing account is acceptable, and if I have more or less accurately described what judges have to do in court when settling questions of human rights, namely to consider what basic moral values are involved, then it follows that the moral is logically prior to the legal. A court of human rights in some sense makes the law, but it does so in the light of a moral judgement.

There is a different way of approaching the question of morality and law that reaches much the same conclusion. This is the theory that the purpose of the criminal law is to enforce, or perhaps reinforce, morality, a theory that was used, as we have seen, to oppose the liberalisation of the law against male homosexuality in the mid-1960s. Obviously, if this account of the criminal law is right, then the concept of morality must be in some sense logically prior to that of at least the criminal law.

It is indeed possible to imagine a Utopia in which everyone was so virtuous, so morally impeccable, so filled with loving kindness that there would be no need for criminal law. There would be need for constitutional law, and civil law laying down the proper way to draw up wills, make contracts, define property and generally conduct the business of life, but that would be the whole law. However, human beings are not of that nature, Utopia does not exist, and therefore in the real world criminal laws with their sanctions are needed to govern those who cannot govern themselves. At the same time, it seems impossible to imagine a country, a dystopia, in which the criminal law, if it existed at all, bore no relation to what most people already believed to be right or wrong. In such a state the laws would be disregarded as irrelevant and arbitrary, then denounced, and anarchy or revolution would follow. Again, morality would seem to trump the law.

The neatest way to show the priority of morality is, of course, to appeal to the moral principles that give rise to moral rights, in the process that I have ascribed to judges in human rights cases, above. And probably many judges would appeal openly or covertly to such universal principles, when they make law or 'find' it. These are the principles revealed by God to those of a theological cast of mind, dictated by Nature to French revolutionaries, or by Reason to Plato or to Kant. However, the security of the legal judgment that a right has, or has not, been violated can be no greater than the security of the moral principle that confers the right. It would be difficult for a judge to pronounce with certainty that Diane Pretty had no right to choose her time of death unless he were sure that there exists a universal moral principle that forbids, or at least does not permit, such a choice. (This is why there is a sense in which to talk about human rights is otiose. The same thing could be said by appealing directly to what, morally speaking, is the basis for the judgement that a human right does or does not exist, has or has not been violated.)

However, Lord Devlin, to whose book *The Enforcement of Morals* I have already referred (pp. 10 and 61), has a different argument for the priority of morals. I quoted him as saying that regard for the sanctity of human life, that is the principle that no one should deliberately bring to an end the life of another, is one of the agreed moral principles that binds society together. He argued that, in any society sophisticated enough to have a legal system, there are certain agreed moral prohibitions, and if the legal system does not use its powers and sanctions to uphold these prohibitions, the society will fall apart. It will cease to exist as a society. This is a strong claim. Devlin made it, as I have explained, in the aftermath of the publication of the Wolfenden Report, which recommended decriminalising homosexual acts carried out in private between consenting adult males. The report was based on a liberal theory of law that can be derived from John Stuart Mill, who, in his essay *On Liberty* (1859) argued that the law should have no powers to intervene in a citizen's private life, unless that citizen's actions could be shown to harm others. Devlin, on the other hand, held that most people were outraged by homosexuality, even if not harmed by it, and that this gave opposition to it a status comparable to that of opposition to killing. To permit homosexuality would undermine an agreed prohibition. Liberal laws on this issue would be one of the elements in a legal system that would serve to loosen the bonds of agreed morality, the cement that holds us together.

This position seems extraordinarily implausible in the twenty-first century; but it also shows up serious objections to the theory that the purpose of the criminal law is to enforce a shared and agreed morality. For it suggests, first, that what is truly morally intolerable can be discovered by the degree of shock and disgust that people express at the thought of it. And this is especially alarming in an age when the press and other media can whip up moral outrage with spectacular ease. I certainly do not deny that there is much truth in David Hume's assertion that morality is 'more properly felt than judg'd on'; nor that moral *sentiment* plays a central role in moral judgement. But it is too easy to induce an exaggerated, almost hysterical sentiment, or a sentiment based on partial understanding, for outrage alone to be the measure of how central, or indeed how widely shared, a moral belief is. After all, it is usually the outraged who make the most noise; and it is a press more concerned with circulation than with reasoned judgement that can produce outrage in its own interest.

More seriously, it can be argued that if agreed moral principles are necessary for the preservation of society (as essential, Devlin suggests, as having a government, of whatever sort) then it seems not to matter what the content of this morality is, or what its principles enjoin or forbid, as long there are some principles or other that people share. Thus the extreme excesses of anti-Semitism, or racial segregation, could be justified as long as these shared prejudices bind a society together. We hardly need to be reminded how indoctrination and propaganda can cement such bonds.

I have to admit that in 1985, when I was retrospectively attempting a philosophical justification of the recommendations of the Report on Human Fertilisation and Embryology (*A Question of Life*, Blackwell 1985, p. xiff.], and specifically explaining the reasoning by which the Committee had reached its controversial conclusion – that research using human embryos should be permitted, subject to regulation – I found myself using arguments close to those of Lord Devlin. I was at that time inclined to the view that any civil society had a shared concept of certain moral barriers that must in no circumstances be crossed. For the most part, one could ascertain where these barriers lay by consulting the criminal law, which had itself been built up to protect society against their being crossed But in a new field of enterprise (such as might be thought to have opened up with the first successful heart transplant, for example, as well as the first successful fertilisation of a human embryo in the laboratory), it would be the business of the criminal law to erect new barriers, compatible, as far as possible, with the rest of society's shared moral taboos. What was essential was that there should be some barrier or other, the crossing of which should be a criminal offence, and which yet seemed only a reasonable extension of current moral ideas. Thus the Committee of Inquiry, as I have already explained, and as I then argued, drew a line that prohibited the use of embryos in research after 14 days from fertilisation. The line was not exactly arbitrary: there were developmental reasons that made 14 days a plausible cutting-off point for research. But the crucial thing was to have a barrier of some kind or other so that moral outrage could be avoided. I did not go as far as Lord Devlin in saying that society would fall to pieces if such taboos were not enshrined and enforced by law, but nevertheless I relied on the idea of pre-existing agreed principles of morality that somehow defined the kind of society of which one wished to be a part. And 'one' meant pretty well everyone who thought about it.

I still believe that there is something in this notion. If it is discovered, for example, that torture has been officially used, or its use sanctioned, on suspected terrorists, then most people's feeling is one of profound shame, moral shame at being part of a society that would allow such a thing to happen. No arguments based on the utility of the information thus acquired or the need to extract confessions and find culprits could weigh against this outrage. Whether we say there is a human right not to be tortured, or simply that it is profoundly morally wrong to subject anyone to torture, does not matter. What we immediately want is for the law to be made more explicit, the sanctions attached more severe, and the monitoring more scrupulous, so that torture can be stamped out. But I am more sceptical than I used to be about the extent that moral consensus exists or can be achieved, still less assumed. And this is perhaps the justification for introducing the concept of human rights. For the language of rights at least sounds 'objective', as if what was a right (or the violation of a right) could be established as a matter of agreed fact, not subject to variation or difference of opinion. It interweaves the law more closely into morality, perhaps for the benefit of both. Moreover, while Lord Devlin's argument relied on an agreed morality within a particular society, the very existence of which was threatened by disregarding it, the language of human rights is universal, the rights being derived from humanity itself, no matter of what society the human beings might be a part.

However, I still hold, like Bentham, that morals and law must be conceptually separated, so that we may criticise the law on moral grounds. For example, even if the law were changed to permit people to take their suffering relatives to Switzerland to die, I believe it would be a morally unsatisfactory law, because inequitable. Only the rich could afford to take advantage of it. More important, it would fudge the genuinely moral question, which needs to be answered before the law is changed, namely whether assisting someone to die is ever morally justifiable. If, as many people hold, to help someone to commit suicide is not only illegal in this country but also immoral (ultimately, illegal because immoral), it would be paradoxical to think that it would not still be immoral if carried out in Switzerland. It cannot be morally right, or even permissible just so long as it is not carried out in our backyard. The DPP's guidance seems to suggest that in the cases where he would be unlikely to prosecute – that is, where the motive was compassionate, and the terminally ill patient was found genuinely to wish for death – then the act of assisting suicide can be morally justified. Yet it remains a crime. So is it wrong or is it not? This is the great moral question that is left unanswered. If assisted dying is, in some circumstances, to be morally justified then the law of this country needs to tackle the matter afresh, and in the light of moral consensus, if such can be found, must be changed. Morality and law must not be allowed to point in opposite directions.

Yet moral consensus on this question does not exist, and never will, certainly as long as the Churches teach that to help someone to achieve the death they long for is the same as murder, and as long as some people heed that teaching, while others do not. It seems that we must look in vain for the great principles that act as the cement holding society together, which Lord Devlin discerned. So how can the kinds of essentially moral issues such as I have been discussing in the last chapters ever be satisfactorily settled? There are some moral questions about which it seems one will always have to admit different opinions. How can the law reflect and follow in the footsteps of morality, if the moral sensibility of society is deeply, and apparently irrevocably, divided?

Nevertheless, though consensus may be impossible to reach in the case of some moral questions, there is, all the same, a huge degree of agreement in the public at large about other questions. And a democratically elected parliament is the best interpreter of where this consensus lies, and how it may in the end be reached. For, as was probably the case when capital punishment was abolished, an elected parliament may sometimes lead moral opinion, and produce consensus where none existed before.

And this leads to what is the crucial point of this whole discussion of the relation between morality and the law of the land. The greatest moral consensus of all, perhaps the nearest to Lord

Devlin's cement that holds society together, is that we, all of us, need and therefore want the security of living under the rule of law. The great jurist, Albert Venn Dicey (*Law of the Constitution*, 1885), defined the rule of law as containing three elements: the absolute predominance of regular law, so that government has no arbitrary authority over the citizen; the equal subjection of all (including officials) to the ordinary law, administered by the ordinary courts; and the fact that the citizen's personal freedoms are formulated and protected by the ordinary law, not by abstract constitutional declarations. I have argued in this chapter that there is a sense in which morality is prior to, lies behind and is the foundation of the law. And I strongly believe this to be true. Yet it is to the law that we give an authority that morality alone, however sincerely upheld and widely agreed, cannot have. And this authority, which comes not merely from the sanctions that must be attached to the law, but from the agreed process by which it became law, is what gives law its predominance, which is different from logical priority. If law did not have this unique authority arising from the due process by which it was enacted and subsequently administered in the courts, then it would be possible for parliamentarians or indeed judges or prime ministers to make laws arbitrarily. It would further be possible for anyone to claim, if they were brave enough, that their moral principles entitled them to disregard the law. But if they did so, they would still have to acknowledge that they must accept the penalties that the law would exact. For, as Dicey says, the rule of law means that the law applies to everyone; there is no one who is above the law, whatever their moral principles or their powers, ecclesiastical or secular, may be.

The general moral convictions of society may change. This happened in the case of abortion, the wrongs of unwanted pregnancy leading to backstreet terminations, and the entitlement of women to have some choice came, in the view of most people, to outweigh the wrong of the destruction of a foetus, and in the end this change in moral attitude brought about a change in the law. A law will find its authority eroded where it has become too restrictive of what has come to seem a proper freedom, or has otherwise fallen out of line with society. Yet all that anyone, ordinary citizen or legislator or judge, can do is to argue the case for change, on broadly moral grounds. Once change comes, it will involve all the ordinary means by which laws are made and enforced, and it is this that gives the law its authority.

CHAPTER FOUR

Morality and Religion: Where Morality Comes From

In the preceding chapters I have considered some examples of what may be called 'moral' legislation, and I have concentrated especially on recent legislation (or attempts to legislate) concerned with birth and death, in which people's moral convictions are deeply involved, whatever the origins of these convictions. I have argued that, while the law is based on morality, the concept of morality being in some sense prior to and necessarily informing the concept of law, there is also a sense in which law has more authority than morality, and that the moral principle upon which society most completely depends is the principle of the rule of law, which is the recognition of that authority. This principle is entirely secular, being based on human necessity rather than on any particular religious doctrine. If we are to live in society at all, that society must recognise the authority of its own laws and their universal and equal application. However, in democratic societies these laws may be changed in accordance with changing values, new knowledge and newly perceived risks. An illustration of such changes can be found in the developing statutes that create the entitlement of all children to education, and those that increasingly seek to safeguard their enjoyment of proper freedoms and proper care in residential homes and boarding schools. Legislators, in making new laws, are envisaging a future that will be, in some particular aspect, better than the past; and in doing so will obviously appeal to moral values other than that of the supremacy of law itself. It is these values that will constitute the justification for any changes that are made. In the examples I have just cited, society's attitude towards children has changed over the centuries, their well-being and happiness being taken more seriously, and the law has been changed accordingly.

We have seen that it is, in practice, very difficult to separate the roles that religion and secular morality play in this moral foundation, upon which new or reforming legislation, or indeed opposition to it, is based. This is partly because of the immense and continuing influence that broadly Christian morality has on our society. It is partly because few parliamentarians, even if they are known to have deep religious convictions, base their arguments entirely on their faith, or the theological framework of their worldview. For people who profess a religion and who live in a community within which religious beliefs are tolerated and respected, the concept of religion as the chief source of morality is hardly questioned. Even those who have given up religious belief themselves often nevertheless assume that for others, who retain their religion, its main point is the morality it teaches. Yet it is of the greatest importance to separate the idea of religion from that of morality. Monotheistic religions define the morally good life as the life of obedience to God's will; or at least the life of loving God, and consequently loving one's neighbour. The good cannot be conceived without reference to the supernatural. For secular morality, on the other hand, the good life is lived according to values derived from the nature of humanity itself.

The importance of making this distinction is, first, that there are many people for whom religion means nothing at all. They can hardly be described as atheists, because, for them, the concept of either believing or not believing in God is simply absent.

An atheist is properly one who recognises that some people believe something that he or she denies, namely that God exists. For many people the question whether God exists or not does not seriously arise. They are totally indifferent to, and, increasingly, ignorant of, any religious ideas including that of God. But as long as they think, however vaguely, that to speak of moral virtues or vices, of moral obligations or betrayals, is necessarily connected with religious belief, then the danger is that they will dismiss the whole lot together, religion and morality alike. If they hear the language of morality spoken, they will regard it, like Thrasymachus in Plato's *Republic*, as a trick played by the stronger on the weaker, an elaborate but meaningless set of rules devised to keep the underdog in his place; nothing will seem to lie behind it or justify it except what they dismiss as the unintelligible mumbo-jumbo that makes up religious discourse. Religion and morality are together one big fairy tale. Those who profess religious faith, and those of the clergy who are unable to discuss moral issues without reference to God, do a great disservice to society, insofar as they prevent moral questions being taken seriously except by those who share their own beliefs.

Second, we all know, and are constantly reminded, that we live in a multifaith, multicultural society, and that discrimination against anyone for their religious beliefs is a punishable offence. What particular faith you have, if any, is widely seen as a matter of personal choice or family background (thus, we are told, we must respect people of 'all faiths and none'). If faith and morality are indissolubly linked together, then it will seem to follow that morality too is a matter of free choice. What is held good by one person may be held bad by another, all good and evil depending on your particular point of view. More damaging still, people may come to think that, as religion is optional, so morality is optional likewise. Those who hold such a view are strictly amoral, without morality. Morality can be simply dismissed, just as God has been. It does not have to be an element in any decision-making, and it can exercise no restraints on conduct. If God is dead, anything is possible.

There is a further risk, namely that those who would defend religion as the necessary source of morality will become fanatical, intolerant and fundamentalist, and therefore more dangerous. The fear of total moral relativism, or of amoralism, is very deep; and in response to it there are those who cling to the apparently absolute and immovable rock of religious texts. Indeed it may be that, considering the world as a whole, the influence of religion is greater than it has been for many years, an increasing rather than a diminishing force in society. But it is the most dogmatic, literal and evangelical forms of religious belief that tend to survive in a world that is largely secular and morally insecure. Yet even if in some respects religion is gaining influence in its extreme forms, influence must not be mistaken for authority; and we need no reminding how disastrous the consequences can be of allowing authority to the dogmas of fundamentalist religion.

It is for these reasons that I want now to try to effect a conceptual separation of religion from morality, and to suggest a secure foundation for morality that safeguards it from relativism. However, first it is necessary to emphasise the obvious point, already noticed, that the Christian religion has had an enormous influence on the values incorporated in the law in this country, an influence that is lasting and will never go away, however secular society becomes. There were centuries during which it would have been impossible to make the conceptual separation that I want to make: it is history that has so entangled religion with morality as expressed in the law. Lord Justice Denning used to say: 'I use the little aphorism "without religion there can be no morality, and without morality there can be no law".' In his view, expressed, for example, in the 33rd Earl Grey Lecture delivered at Newcastle-upon-Tyne in 1953 (cited in Edmund Heward, *Lord*

Denning: A Biography, Barry Rose Law Publishers 2002, p. 103),
the law proceeds on the Christian principles of justice and fairness: 'Religion concerns the spirit in man whereby he is able to
recognise what is truth and what is justice; whereas the law is
only the application, however imperfectly, of truth and justice in
our everyday affairs.' And he believed that people are taught to
distinguish justice from injustice, good from evil, by the Church,
as he had been. It is only in the light of this teaching, he believed,
that legislators may reform and judges interpret the law. Denning
was probably the last to uphold an old tradition according to
which it was simply assumed that morality derived from Christianity, and judges, whether they knew it or not, were acting under
the power of religion.

Things have changed. However, there has recently been a revival
of something like Lord Denning's old-fashioned view that only
religion can provide the moral certainty that must lie behind the
law. It is plain, for one thing, that in the USA religion and politics
are far more closely interwoven than in this country (though not
more so than in some predominantly Roman Catholic countries,
such as Ireland and Italy) and this despite the fact that the found-
ing fathers separated church from state, largely in order to protect freedom for religion, the ideal in pursuit of which many of
them had left home. The consequence of this was the formation
of numerous different, independent nonconformist sects, which
in turn has now issued in a huge rise in fundamentalist Christianity. Such religious beliefs, sometimes bizarre in their literal
interpretation of the scriptures and their denial of scientific
facts, are essentially concerned with clean, healthy and upright
living, ideals especially admired by 'good Americans'. Consequently, it would be difficult for an American politician to dis-
avow any attachment to a church, especially in middle America,
in the Bible Belt, but more generally as well. It is doubtful if anyone could become an elected Congressman or Senator, let alone

President, who did not profess a religious belief, or belong to some church. And it is apparently less important that the content of religious belief should be coherent than that some religious belief or other should be professed. (How great the intellectual dishonesty involved in this widespread profession of faith it is difficult for a non-American to assess.)

In any case, in this country a rather more sophisticated claim for the necessity and indeed the priority of religion in politics is starting to be heard. Theology has begun to challenge secular 'liberal' political philosophy, which is presented as over-materialistic and too much tied up within the market economy, wedded to the individual's right to accumulate wealth. The rot of secularisation began, on this view, with Bentham, who, as we have seen, rejected the concept of a divine law above the laws of actual states, and who adopted a purely human standard both of right and wrong and of good laws and bad: the standard of the greatest happiness of the greatest number. His criterion was human well-being, not obedience to the divine will. (There had in fact been atheistical political theorists before Bentham, such as Thomas Hobbes (1588–1678), who held that obedience to the rule of law was necessary but entirely in the interest of human beings themselves since without it their lives would revert to the state of nature: nasty, brutish and short.)

According to the new theologico-political theory, known as Radical Orthodoxy, what has been sacrificed to the capitalist god has been the idea of fairness and, more important still, that of community. Marxism, the ideology above all others that sought to prove the evils of capitalism and destroy it, has failed in practice; and the Radical theologians claim that people who might once have been Marxists are turning to Christian theology for salvation. The new movement may be exemplified by the writings of John Milbank, currently Professor of Religion, Politics and Ethics at the University of Nottingham, to whose work I shall come shortly.

But before that, it is necessary to say something about his recent predecessors. There have long been members of the Christian churches who have seen their Christian mission as an attempt to live a Christ-like life among the poor, the exploited and the dispossessed, and who would not have denied that their mission was also political, and that it entitled them to pronounce on matters of social policy. Their theology was sometimes called Incarnation theology, since they claimed to seek out and recognise God in Man, wherever there was suffering, at home or abroad. I remember a certain Canon of Winchester Cathedral, Roger Lloyd, from the late 1930s onwards (much influenced, I now see, by Archbishop William Temple), who preached with passion that theology was action, and that no one could claim to believe in God who did not work among the poor; that the whole of the gospel speaks of nothing except equality, and that the money-lenders must again have their tables overturned. The niceties of theology, the traditions and hierarchies of church and cathedral, were of no importance in his eyes. Christ was to be found only in the inner cities. I used to hear him preach during the war, especially in 1941, at the time of the publication of the Beveridge Report, when everyone was full of the great changes to come as soon as war was over. This was Christian Socialism, and was much disliked by my mother and her friends, who disapproved of the politicisation of religion as much as I disapprove of the theologising of politics. The gossips around the Close delighted to calculate Canon Lloyd's income (he was also a prolific journalist, writing mainly about trains, and a novelist) and the value of his exquisite canon's residence. He was a powerful, and powerfully guilt-inducing, preacher, who – with his pale face and narrow head wobbling from side to side in his emotion – was a familiar figure, much admired by me in my teens.

But the new Radical Orthodoxy is different from Christian Socialism (and far less intelligible). The present Archbishop of

Canterbury, Dr Rowan Williams, may be seen as a kind of bridge between the old social Christianity and the new Radicalism (he was John Milbank's theological tutor). In an essay entitled 'Interiority and Epiphany' (Rowan Williams, *On Christian Theology*, Basil Blackwell 2000, chapter 16, pp. 263ff.), he wrote this:

'Christian "bias to the poor" is not simply a doctrine that God likes poor people better than others, and that is all there is to it. It is rather a persistent critical concern about how claims to do with security and legitimation are made, both in and out of the Church. It is a "bias" in the sense that the Christian begins with a non-negotiable commitment to basic egalitarianism.'

And he goes on later, speaking of the language of individual rights, to say this:

'... [the language of rights] becomes sterile when it is divorced from a proper conception of the human good that has to be worked on in conversation with others. In this sense... Christian ethics is relentlessly political because it cannot be adequately expressed in terms of atomized rights vested in individuals or groups, but looks beyond to the kind of community in which free interaction for the sake of each other is made possible. That means adjustment and listening; it means politics.'

Thus, according to the Archbishop, religion must be part of the dialogue and the compromises of politics, and its voice will always be heard to defend equality, the inclusion of all within society, as its highest value. This is its specifically Christian starting point; but it is also the justification for democratic political institutions. It follows, according to the Archbishop, that religion has full justification for adopting a political role and making its voice heard in Parliament.

Rowan Williams's pupil, however, insofar as he is capable of being understood, seems to go much further. In his book of collected essays, written over a period of about thirty years (*The Future of Love: Essays in Political Theology*, SCM Press, 2009), John Milbank sets out from the proposition that 'the welfare of this world has been wrecked by the ideology of neoliberalism, and yet its historic challengers, conservatism and socialism, have been mostly in total disarray' (p. 242). In the central essay from which this quotation is taken ('Liberality versus Liberalism', pp. 242ff.), Milbank argues that socialism, previously readily linked with if not derived from Christianity, has been overtaken by the new liberalism (exemplified, presumably, in the invention of New Labour) within which greed and crude materialistic utilitarianism has overcome any concern for equality. So he proposes that there must be a new 'openness to religion in political theory'. Religion, and especially Christianity, would, he argues, supply new fundamental concepts that could revolutionise politics.

The first of these concepts is the idea of the gift, as opposed to the contract, as the proper foundation of communal activity; and this entails that love – not justice or equal rights – is, or should be, the binding force within society. This leads him into strange political fields, some of them reminiscent of the version of socialism advocated by, for example, the Catholic writer Hillaire Belloc, sometimes known as Collectivism: politics on a small scale, capital vested in a community, with property distributed within the community, everyone with his acre and a cow. Milbank insists, at any rate, on the principle that political responsibility must be vested in local organisations, with people's livelihoods as far as possible based on local production. Communities must be felt to be such, and thus must be small. Only within small communities can there be an intelligible concept of a common good, of people working together for each other, the central Christian idea of love. Throughout this and other essays (insofar as I have been able to understand them, for they are peculiarly difficult for non-theologians to follow) there is one recurring theme: 'Where there is no public recognition of the primacy of absolute good as grounded in something super-human then democracy becomes impossible, for it is no longer supposed that one should even *search* for the intrinsically desirable.' Milbank argues that in a secular democracy, people can find out what they ought to desire (what is desirable) only from themselves, and their fellow democrats, that is from what people generally *do* desire. So liberal democracy is nothing but populism. It is rather as if what you ought to want, say what music you ought to want to listen to, can be determined only by a published 'chart', which shows you the top-ten most purchased recordings every week. And this of course not only brings about a kind of herd behaviour, but is easily manipulable for commercial gain. So it is, holds Milbank, with democracy, unless people can be given some proper standard by which to discriminate the good from the bad, the intrinsically desirable from the fluctuating, merely fashionable or actually undesirable. And this standard must be supernatural. His conclusion is that 'the only true justification of democracy must be theological'.

Plainly the assumption, never properly examined, that lies behind this conclusion is that there can be no standard of what is right, no meaningful concept of what is good, that is not 'grounded in something superhuman'. Now such a belief could lead to an assertion that for a reliable and objective standard of what is good to exist, there must also exist a kind of Platonic, unchanging Idea of the Good, a view espoused by Iris Murdoch in her neo-Platonist writings (see, for example, *The Sovereignty of Good*, Routledge 1991, *passim*, but especially chapter 2, 'On "God" and "Good"'). 'Goodness', according to such a theory, could be said in some sense to exist, but would not possess any of the attributes of 'God'; especially, it would be totally impersonal, would not know or care for individual human beings, nor be their creator. Such a view is not considered by Milbank, who goes straight to the conclusion that a belief in God, the God of Christianity, the creator of man and of the moral law, is necessary for morality, and hence for politics.

The belief that parliamentarians must accept what it is that they 'ought to desire' from a higher, transcendental or supernatural source has always been characteristic also of the Roman Catholic Church, and has posed great difficulties for individual Roman Catholic MPs in recent cases of 'moral' legislation. This was nowhere clearer than in the passage through Parliament of the Human Fertilisation and Embryology Act (2008), an update of the 1990 Act which we have already considered. The Act of 2008 regulates the use of human embryos outside the uterus, however they came into being, whether through normal fertilisation *in vitro*, or through the process of 'therapeutic cloning' (see pp. 35–36); it permits human admixed embryos created for purposes of research by a combination of human material and that from other animals; it formally lifts the restriction of IVF treatment to heterosexual couples, and it omits the provision in the original Act that, before providing IVF treatment to a woman, the child's 'need for a father' must be taken into account. It is, in short, a paradigm case of liberalising legislation.

It had been the intention of the Prime Minister, Gordon Brown, that, this being a Government Bill, all votes would be on party lines, and there should be no free or 'conscience' vote. But the representations of various Roman Catholic members of the Cabinet, and some junior ministers, forced him to remove the whip. These Roman Catholics were not acting simply on their own conscience, however imbued that conscience might be with Roman Catholic doctrine; they had been positively instructed that they must oppose these provisions of the Bill. In a doctrinal note published in 2002, the Vatican had pronounced that 'while democracy is the best expression of the direct participation of citizens in political choices, it succeeds only to the extent that it is based on a correct understanding of the human *person*. Catholic involvement in political life cannot compromise on this principle.' The note was specifically directed not only to bishops but to

all those who took part in public debate or who had public political responsibility. 'Catholics have not only a right but a duty to
oppose any legislation that undermines the sanctity of life from
conception to natural death.' Here, then, is a statement echoed by
John Milbank, though he writes as an Anglican, not a Roman
Catholic. Democracy is to be defended only insofar as it is
founded upon theological doctrine. Only so can individual parliamentarians know what it is that they 'ought to desire'.

In my view, such a role for theology is profoundly wrong, and
I believe that it is necessary to reinstate secular morality as the
basis for introducing new legislation and for the criticism and
amending of existing law. But before engaging with this matter
directly, I must first say something about what may perhaps be
thought to be a little local difficulty relating to parliamentary
proceedings in this country alone, and raising no philosophical
issues. This, of course, is the existence in the House of Lords of
the Bishops' Bench. Elizabeth Wicks, senior lecturer in Medical
Law at the University of Birmingham, in an article published in
the *Medical Law Review* in 2009, has argued that the presence
of the bishops as part of the legislating body obscures the true
nature of the moral arguments that must be seriously addressed
in debates on 'moral legislation'. Writing about the House of
Lords debate on the Assisted Dying Bill in 2006, she says this:

'there is a legitimate cause for concern over the role of the bishops in
legislating on complex moral issues … Many lords spoke as Christians
(or Muslims or Jews or Atheists), and it is right that they should do so,
for their religious faith (or the lack thereof) will inevitably feed into their
conclusions on ethical issues such as assisted dying, but it is not solely a
religious issue. Much less is it solely an issue for religious leaders. The
high-profile presence of the Church of England bishops in the House of
Lords for this debate [and the Bishops' Bench was conspicuously
crowded] distracts from the multi-faceted ethical debate that should
surround any proposal to legislate for assisted dying because it presents
a superficial view of the objections to such a proposal. ('Religion, Law

and Medicine: Legislating on Birth and Death in a Christian State',
Medical Law Review 17, p. 410)

She goes on to quote an article by Polly Toynbee in the
Guardian (12 May 2006), where she speaks of a cabal of bishops,
rabbis, imams, evangelists and other believers organising a coup
against the bill. Elizabeth Wicks says that perceptions such as this,
of religious peers single-handedly preventing the Bill's passage

'may not only undermine potentially valid secular objections to the
Bill, but also serve to deny all validity to genuine religious objections. It
is the idiosyncratic presence of religious representatives in the modern
legislature, more than the religious opposition itself, that encourages
such extreme and damaging perceptions, while the true ethical debate
becomes obscured.' (*Ibid.*)

She would therefore abolish the right of bishops to sit as part
of a legislating body (though she would not object, I suppose, to
some bishops becoming life peers, in virtue of their general suit-
ability for that role, for then they would sit not as representatives
of the Church, but as individual Christians).

To debar the bishops from membership of the House of Lords
in virtue of their office would not necessarily entail the disestab-
lishment of the Church of England, for the bishops could still
take it in turns to say prayers before sittings, and could perform
other ceremonial functions connected with the monarchy and
the judiciary. So the issue is not whether or not the Church of
England should be disestablished (and I do not believe that it
should, however disunited, precarious and lacking in standing
it may temporarily have become). The question is whether the
presence of the bishops within Parliament, as a group represent-
ing the Church, has undue influence on the outcome of debates
on legislation concerned with moral matters.

Now it is true that the convention in the House of Lords is
that if anyone gets up to speak at the same time as a bishop, that
other peer will defer to the Right Reverend Prelate (the bishops

are, however, careful never to get up if a front-bench peer from any party wishes to intervene). And I do not deny that this is sometimes irritating. It is true, too, that when they speak they obviously speak as religious believers. How could they not? But then, so do other peers; there are at least two rabbis in the House of Lords, several retired bishops and archbishops, and many people who declare themselves as believers. However, as I have already remarked, most of these peers – including the bishops who have been created life peers and are cross-benchers – say very little if anything about what their faith tells them, or elaborate in detail on what part their faith has played in the formation of their moral beliefs, and some, as we have seen, deliberately try to separate their religious from their moral convictions. In the debates on the Assisted Dying Bills, for example, nearly all of these peers who spoke, including those from the Bishops' Bench, after perhaps a nodding reference to the predominantly religious argument from the sanctity of human life, went on immediately to use purely secular arguments derived from the disastrous consequences that they foresaw if the law were changed, arguments used equally by the godly and the ungodly alike. I agree with Elizabeth Wicks when she says that it is not the religious opposition in itself that is objectionable; such opposition is proper and legitimate. I disagree with her, however, when she says that what is wrong is that the bishops represent the Anglican Church. In my view, the mischief lies rather in the assumption on the part of most peers that because the bishops are religious professionals, they are therefore moral experts. It is in their supposed role as experts, experts not in theology but in morals, that they are attended to with such deference. This has a doubly bad effect. First, it means that many peers fail to take seriously their fellows who are atheists or humanists or who, while professing a faith, yet try to separate dogmatic from practical, or indeed private from public morality. They are thought not to be qualified to speak. Second, it serves to reinforce the confusion between religion and morality, which is intrinsically dangerous for reasons which I have already, in part at least, adduced. While no one could seriously hold that any religious beliefs whatever, however dotty or perverse, will give rise to moral opinions worthy of respect, there is nevertheless a tendency to speak as if Faith were in itself good, so-called People of Faith being somehow joined together in a common moral enterprise. And so they often are, insofar as they are part of a long tradition, not only among Christians but among other religions too, of caring for such things as education and the relief of poverty and disease. But often they are not; and we do not have to search very hard to find evidence of religious faith that is conjoined with barbarous moral beliefs and flagrantly illegal activity.

In April 2007 Lord Harrison – a Labour peer, and a forthright and generous man well known for his philanthropy as well as for his passion for architecture and education – introduced a Thursday Debate (not for the passage of legislation, but for the discussion of matters of current concern) 'To call attention to the position in Britain of those who profess no religion'. His contention was that government policy to encourage all the faiths to cooperate with one another and with the government for the same social ends discriminated unfairly against those who belonged to no faith. The policy had formed part of the Labour manifesto of 2001, and issued in a government paper entitled *Working Together*, and another entitled *Building Civil Renewal*, where religious groups had powers delegated to them for work within the community, especially in inner cities. Almost any religious group, however small, eccentric and obscure, such as the Jains and Zoroastrians, might be so privileged, while no such powers and responsibilities were proffered to those who, equally minded to help their community, held no faith. (In her reply, the then Under-Secretary of State, in the Department of Communities and Local Government, the amiable Baroness Andrews, assured him that the point of the government paper *Working Together* was only to encourage faith groups to work in communities with which they often have a unique relationship, not to exclude others from doing so, or from tendering for the provision of local services.) Many peers agreed with Lord Harrison, especially in the matter of state-funded church schools which may refuse to enrol children whose parents are not churchgoers. Some who were non-believers, on the other hand, felt no sense of being unjustly discriminated against and did not want to be categorised as a new group – say, perhaps, the Humanists. It fell to Lord Joffe, not surprisingly, to address the question whether within Parliament itself, and in matters of legislation, the godly had undue power over the godless. His point was that parliamentarians, even members of the House of Lords who have no constituents to consider, are subject to lobbying, and their votes on any matter may be swayed by the intensity of the lobby, especially if the letters and briefings they receive purport to be backed up by statistics that show the views of the public outside Parliament. In the case of his last Bill to legalise assisted dying for the terminally ill, the lobbying was unprecedented. It was initiated by Archbishop Peter Smith, the Catholic Archbishop of Cardiff, who announced that he was launching the biggest political campaign by the Church in its whole modern history. Questionnaires were sent out to highly selective groups, so that a huge majority was shown to be hostile to the Bill. The campaign culminated in an article published in the *Catholic Times* on 2 April 2006, entitled 'Legalising Euthanasia turns Carers into Killers', which included a photograph of 24 children who had been murdered by the Nazis in the late 1930s. Lord Joffe was not pleased. He said (*Hansard* HL, 19 April 1997, cols 357–358]: 'The faith groups' campaign was a great victory, as the Bill was defeated at Second Reading by the breach of a long-standing tradition never to oppose a Private Member's Bill at

Second Reading, and by the ignoring of the key recommendations of the Select Committee which the House had set up to consider the Bill.' The outcome, he said, was that a Bill which other opinion polls had shown to be supported by 80 per cent of the public was defeated by 'a campaign orchestrated by the churches'. Of course peers need not have paid any attention to their lobbying post, especially as the letters were entirely formulaic, not the outcome of individual thought but written by a central source and merely signed by the sender; and indeed I suspect that Lord Joffe, certainly suffering a sense of persecution, exaggerated the influence that this less than honest campaign had on the recipients of the letters. There was, as I have outlined already, fierce opposition to his Bill not only from the churches, but also from those other great monolithic obstacles in the path of reform, Medicine and the Law. Nevertheless I believe that the conflation of religion and morality, and the habit of according moral authority to the declarations of religious leaders, played a considerable part in the refusal of a Second Reading to this Bill.

So how is this conflation to be avoided? How is the separation of morals from religious faith to be brought about? It is clear that one of the things that chiefly drives people into demanding and clinging to a superhuman foundation for morality is the fear that without it there will be no possibility of agreement on ethical issues. Moral standards, if any survive, will be totally random, as changeable as fashion and therefore as trivial. Moral relativism denies the possibility of certainty and permanence in moral judgements; it reduces them to the status of personal preference, or personal interest, not even aspiring to the solidity and stability of truth. We live in a culture of tolerance, or at least in a culture where tolerance, even if not practised, is regarded as a virtue. We also know well how enormously various the beliefs, superstitions and taboos are, even among people who live on our doorstep, and we are taught that we must respect them all. Criticism of

them, if too loud, can lead not just to disapproval but to prosecution. Teachers are deeply afraid of failing to show complete even-
handedness. Such careful refusal to pass moral judgements leads
to moral vacillation and confusion. It is no wonder that people
seek the embrace of a dogmatic and self-justifying Faith, even if
adopting it, or clinging to its familiarity, entails assenting to
propositions which they do not actually believe, or which if literally interpreted contradict both science and history.

But moral relativism is not new. We should perhaps look at it
more closely, to see whether it is as powerful an enemy as it
seems, if we are to try to find a form of morality that is able to
stand up by itself, without its origin in God's will or its support
in Faith. Aristotle was aware that some people thought of ethics
as subject to such variability and fluctuating changes that it was a
matter only of convention, with no stable nature of its own. All
depended on when and where you lived (Aristotle, *Nicomachaean
Ethics*, Book I, 1094b12). Disagreeing with this, he said that,
nevertheless, one should seek only as much certainty and accuracy as the subject-matter allowed. Ethics, the pursuit of the
good, was, after all, concerned with real happenings in the real
world, which cannot be wholly predictable. One must be content
with propositions that are 'for the most part true'. (This is why he
thought it not a suitable subject for the young. It needs knowledge of people and of how things actually are. For the young,
mathematics was a better study (*Nicomachaean Ethics*, Book I,
1095a3)). I think we should heed these words. Moral conviction
is no more subject to proof than the convictions of faith. Morality, however, has the advantage that it is concerned with the
world we live in, and the people with whom we have dealings. We
know from experience what it is like to be helped when we are in
trouble, or, on the other hand, to be deceived or betrayed. We can
look about us for evidence of the value to people of some things,
the disvalue of others. Moral judgements and decisions, while

concerned with the here and now, are also crucially about what we think will be the future, for ourselves and others, if we decide this way or that, and we learn to make this kind of judgement from experience.

Some people hope that an agreed and stable morality and a proper foundation for legislation can be found in the concept of human rights. I have said enough above to show that I do not believe that this is so, even though the concept of what is to count as a violation of universal human rights is becoming more widely accepted and therefore more useful. But to speak of a human right is in fact only a kind of shorthand by which to refer to a moral principle concerning how people should or should not be treated, and thus a human right, even an inalienable right, cannot be the foundation of morality.

Moreover, the idea of a right has another, fundamental flaw, and one which sometimes makes it seem actually in conflict with the concept of morality itself. A right is something that can be claimed and defended against infringement by another person. It is an area of freedom, or of possession, for an individual which someone else, or some group, must allow to be exercised, as a matter of justice. Thus if someone successfully claims something as a right this entails that there exists someone else, or some group of other people, who has the duty to ensure that he or she can exercise their right. People often say, carelessly, that rights entail duties, meaning that if you are aware of your rights you ought to be aware of your duties as well. But, though this may be a morally respectable thing to say, it entirely distorts the actual logical connection between rights and duties. There is no logical connection between my rights and my duties; my rights are rights against others (however vaguely defined) who are obliged to secure me in the exercise of my rights. After all, infants may be thought to have rights which can be claimed on their behalf, but they can have no duties. In a civilised society it may be held that even the most powerless have a right to food and shelter; and then it becomes the duty of society or the state to provide it. Neglecting this logical connection results in meaningless proclamations of universal rights, such as the UNICEF *Declaration of the Rights of the Child*, published in 1990, which the UK signed and ratified, and which sets out a number of ideals for the way it is desirable for children to be brought up, being educated, living with their families, having time to play and exercise their imaginations in the arts, and other good things. These are doubtless very nice and indeed very good as ideals, even perhaps effective as rhetoric, but nobody in particular has or could have a duty to ensure that they are fulfilled.

Worse even than this is the fact that, as I have said, the concept of rights depends on the concept of justice, of what each individual person is owed. But morality cannot be derived from nothing except the idea of justice, important though this idea may be in a moral society. Avoiding injustice, though central to the value we ascribe to the rule of law, is not the only moral value. To be a truly moral person, it is necessary, as well, to avoid cruelty, callousness, greed, and many other things that we recognise as vices. More crucially, it is to exercise imagination, to be able to understand the situation of other people, their feelings and their motives, to be capable both of sympathy and of a reasonable judgement of what the consequences of your actions will be, how they will affect other people than yourself. A rights-based morality may of course demand that I recognise not only my own rights, but also the rights of others. (Indeed the law is there to ensure that everyone's rights are equally protected, and can compel me to recognise the rights of others, whether I want to or not.) But this is all that a rights-based morality can do: it cannot embrace what I believe is the essential feature of morality; and that is the ability sometimes to treat others as having not merely an equal but a greater need than I. The morally good person must be prepared at least sometimes to postpone his or her own interests to those of others, to grasp that a situation sometimes demands that they do not claim what is theirs by right, and that there may be values more precious even than that of justice. Justice is a public virtue; it can be a virtue of institutions and legislatures as well as of people. If I claim a right I can in principle take my case to court and hope that I will get a just verdict. The courts have no place for altruism. The victim abandoned in the ditch had no right to be rescued by the Good Samaritan. If he could have claimed a right, the Samaritan, his rescuer, would have been doing no more than his duty; he would not in the same way win our moral admiration, or figure as a moral inspiration. He would be a dutiful but not necessarily an especially good Samaritan.

I have argued already that there is a sense in which the concept of morality must precede the concept of law. This priority is not historical. There can be no *evidence* that people first understood the difference between the morally good and the morally bad, and then set up a society in which the laws reflected this understanding. It is rather that a society that possesses institutions of government and an interest in the rule of law depends on at least some members having goodwill, that is, a wish to do good rather than harm. There must exist people who understand the difference between honesty and corruption, and themselves choose to be honest rather than corrupt, who understand that sometimes they will have to put aside what they immediately want for themselves in order to secure a good that is not their own or not theirs alone. This kind of understanding is what constitutes private morality. If this is so, then it seems to me to follow that it cannot be the notion of individual rights that is the foundation of morality, since a right is itself a quasi-legal concept dependent on nothing except the idea of what is owed, whether to an individual or a group. The idea of not insisting on one's own claims, of recognising, as we used to be taught, that 'one is not the only pebble on the beach', is alien to the claiming of rights, but lies at the heart of morality. It could be objected that the claiming of rights is not necessarily selfish; rights are often claimed and passionately fought for on behalf of others, and this is true. I may certainly demand justice for a group of which I am not myself a member. This may be public-spirited, but it is not altruistic. And justice must be even-handed. If I claim a right for a group of which I am a part, then I am claiming for myself as well. I am saying 'give me what I deserve'. And this, though morally acceptable (if I really do deserve it), cannot be at the centre of our moral ideal. There is, as I have said, more to morality than justice.

So, if not to religion and if not to human rights, where are we to look for a morality that is not, as moral relativism would have it, simply a question of personal preference, no more stable or enduring than fashion? It seems to me that to answer this question, we need to think back to the issues debated during the passage of so-called moral legislation. These were issues of life and death or of human sexuality, issues about which people feel strongly because they are central to their humanity. All these debates and disagreements are to be felt in the guts before they can be legislated upon, and legal rights either established or disallowed. To speak of a pre-existing moral right in such cases (a moral right to have an abortion or to be helped to die), is, as I have already argued, only another way of saying that the law must enact what the legislators believe to be morally best, what, in Milbank's words 'they ought to desire'. If moral relativism is true, then there is no way to find out what they ought to desire, indeed it is senseless to suppose that there is any such thing as what is genuinely and enduringly desirable, or to seek agreement on any such issues.

Yet it seems to me that, however many different customs and taboos people observe, in however many different situations they feel those central moral emotions, shame and pride, those of us, provided we do not suffer from such a personality disorder as to be incapable of forming the concept of morality, know that absolute relativism is not true. We could not live our lives together if we believed that, morally, anything goes. And we know, moreover, that however much Christianity has in the past dominated ethical thinking, secular ethical thinking is not just a leftover from history, borrowing its language from a past that is dead. Some Christian and some atheist philosophers have indeed held that this is so: Elizabeth Anscombe, for example, a Roman Catholic, in an article published in 1958 ('Modern Moral Philosophy', in *Philosophy* 35, 1958) argued that the special and emphatic expressions 'morally ought' and 'morally ought not' could not be given sense without reference to a divine law, permitting, prescribing or forbidding certain conduct, and that the expressions should be dropped by those who did not believe in divine law, to be replaced by the simple 'ought' and 'ought not', which could be given sense by reference to a specific end (such as 'if you want to be safe' or 'if you want to get on in the world'). Similarly, the atheist philosopher John McKie argued in 1977 that morality was no more than a device which had been found useful in the days when the authority of religion could enforce its precepts, and has now been reinvented, borrowing for its vocabulary an authority that properly belonged only to its abandoned origins (see John McKie, *Ethics – Inventing Right and Wrong*, Penguin, 1977). But it seems to me that our experience of actual wrongs, and of actual moral goodness, belies such theories. Ethics need not return to the past in order to come back to life. Aristotle, in the *Nicomachaean Ethics*, claimed that in examining the good for man he was starting from 'the phenomena', what he found to be the case. If we too start from what we see around us, what we know and observe, we can say that there is an enormous difference between good people and bad people, between virtue and vice, between the nice and the nasty. Of course there are differences between the nice and the nasty that are nothing to do with morality at all, such as natural beauty, or natural disasters such as floods and earthquakes, but this does not affect the argument with regard to moral distinctions. We know how to make them, and we do it all the time. As Hume put it

'let a man's insensibility be ever so great, he must often be touched with the images of Right and Wrong; and let his prejudices be ever so obstinate, he must observe that others are susceptible of like impressions. The only way, therefore, of converting an antagonist of this kind [i.e. one who denies the existence of morality] is to leave him to himself.' (David Hume, *An Enquiry concerning the Principles of Morals*, Book I, Section I, para. 133)

Hume thought that morality was concerned with human 'characters and motives'. In this he was surely right. The subject-matter of morality does not encompass natural phenomena, or the behaviour of animals other than human beings, though we may semi-seriously ascribe moral attributes to animals that we know well, and to which we allow both character and motives. But this is anthropomorphism. We are, Hume thought, enabled to distinguish right from wrong by the mechanism of sympathy, through which we feel pleasure in other people's pleasure, and pain in their pain. So if someone has been maliciously injured by another, this causes us pain that arises from the thought of the motive and character of the wrongdoer, and the different pain of sorrow for the suffering of the victim. But Hume recognised that moral judgements are not made on the basis of sympathy alone:

'Nor is every sentiment of pleasure or pain which arises from characters and actions of that *peculiar* kind, which makes us praise or condemn. The good qualities of an enemy are hurtful to us; but may still command our esteem and respect. 'Tis only when a character is considered in general, without reference to our particular interest, that it causes such a feeling or sentiment, as denominates it morally good or evil.' (David Hume, *Treatise of Human Nature*, Book III, Part I, Section II, edited by Selby Bigg, Oxford 1888, p. 472).

And he goes on to say that we may be tempted to ascribe moral turpitude to those who act against our interest, just as we may find it difficult to admire the beautiful voice of someone who has done us an injury, though it in fact gives us a particular musical pleasure. Nevertheless 'a person of fine ear, who has the command of himself, can separate these feelings and give praise to what deserves it' (*ibid.*).

Elsewhere in the Treatise, Hume had spoken of pleasure and pain as simple impressions or experiences, incapable of further analysis, rather as Bentham was later to do in his attempt to establish pleasure and pain as the twin criteria by which alone to judge moral and legal systems. But here Hume shows himself more subtle than Bentham, and in trying to identify and describe the particular pleasure that makes us describe a character or motive as *morally* admirable, he allows that it can arise only when we think not only of ourselves but of human beings in general. I believe that we should take this to heart if we are to find what we are looking for: the basis for a morality that is not purely relative, that is more than a matter of our own personal preferences, and that can stand alone, without the supporting buttress of religion. The sympathy and feeling for others that Hume rightly argues is necessary to give rise to moral distinctions is possible only because two conditions are satisfied. First, human beings must be in fundamental respects alike. Second, they must possess imagination. Both these conditions are assumed by Hume to be satisfied, and I believe that anyone contemplating the phenomenon of morality must make the same assumption. It is through the use of imagination that we can mentally put ourselves in the place of another, and recognise that, because of our common humanity, what is intolerable for another would be intolerable for us also.

Imagination is a central aspect of our mental equipment, and may well be thought the crucial distinguishing feature of human as opposed to other animals. Sartre defined imagination as the ability to think about 'what is not': what is not before our eyes and ears, what does not belong to the present but to the past or the future, what does not exist but is merely possible or hypothetical. This is a fruitful definition. The ability to think about things that are in various ways absent doubtless developed in our ancestors alongside the development of language, and the two are intimately linked. For without language we could not communicate with each other about anything that no longer exists or does not yet exist; or about anything that is not a concrete entity but an abstract idea. It is imagination that allows us to think hypothetically and act on such thoughts. We can envisage not only what would have happened if something had been different; but what may happen if we do this rather than that. It seems to me clear that to be able to think in this way and to articulate such thoughts is essential to the existence of morality. As I have said, to be a moral agent it is necessary to think what the effect of one's behaviour will be on people other than oneself, which involves speculation about possible futures, a thing impossible without imagination. And in morally approving of some outcomes, disapproving of others, we are expressing values: what we regard as agreeable or disagreeable, tolerable or intolerable, nice or nasty.

That such values are to a large extent shared, and expected to be shared, has sometimes been exaggerated by moral philosophers. For example, Franz Brentano (1838–1916) held that among mental phenomena there exist (alongside appearances and judgements) experiences of love and hate, or liking and disliking. Some of the experiences are unquestionable; when we experience such a love or hate, he maintained, we simply know that the object of our feeling is intrinsically good or intrinsically bad. There can be no question of justifying such a reaction: it is its own justification. Thus anybody confronted with the same phenomenon must experience the same awareness of good or evil, nice or nasty.

The Cambridge philosopher and guru of the Bloomsbury group, G. E. Moore (1873–1938), reviewed Brentano's book *The Origins of Ethical Knowledge* when it came out in 1911, and was very much influenced by it. In *Principia Ethica* he expounded the view that goodness was incapable of definition, because it was simple and not made up of separable parts. It could be immediately recognisable and was not to be confused with or derived from any natural characteristics of a thing. One could not justify one's claim that, for example, friendship was good. One just saw that it was so. Brentano and Moore were known as Intuitionists. Their theories were highly implausible, in the light of what we all know about moral (and aesthetic) disagreements. (Moore held that if anyone disagreed with one of his value judgements it was because that person had not thought about the matter clearly.) Nevertheless, they have this insight: all our judgements of good and bad, nice and nasty, take for granted that this is a judgement with which other people could agree. Our specifically moral sentiments are aroused only when other people are taken into account, and we assume that they will to a large extent share our values. My judgement that such and such would be a horrible or an intolerable outcome means horrible for these others who would be affected, not only, sometimes not at all, for me.

Imagination thus enables us to articulate the hypothetical question: 'How would I feel if this happened to me?' (the question one must teach children to ask, if one wants to teach them to behave well towards others rather than badly). And it enables us, through sympathy, to mind about the answer. If I would hate to be badly treated, so would they, and I dislike that thought (or, if I am a child, I should be taught to do so). This once again assumes an identity of values between one person and another, or if not identity then a similarity that renders those values intelligible, between one person and another. Nor should we find this in the least surprising; in fact we take it for granted in real life. We all rejoice in love and friendship; we all detest loss and death and physical pain. If it were not so, we would not have literature or any art that can move us, though it represents nothing that immediately affects our own interests.

It is imagination, too, that enables us to envisage a general, even a global picture, in a way that other animals cannot. This is what I suppose Hume at least partly meant when he spoke of considering a matter in general, without reference to our own particular interests. In the discussion of the putative Kantian lineage of the principle of autonomy (pp. 46–47) I described Kant's Categorical Imperative, derived from reason itself, as requiring us to refrain from doing anything that we could not will to be a universal imperative; or, in other words, to treat every person as entitled to make his or her own rational choices, just as we are entitled, and not to be used as mere means to our own ends. We can take as an example someone who refrains from taking too much for themselves in a situation of scarcity, let us say in a drought, on the grounds that if they did so, in order to satisfy their own desires, they would be relying on other people's observing the water ban. In Kantian terms, they would not only be doing something that they could not will that everyone should do, but they would also be using other people as means to their own ends rather than as rational people like them. Hume would argue, more plausibly, that the man who refrained from using the sprinkler on his lawn during a drought would know that to do so would be wrong, because he could consider his own wish to use water in the general context of other people as well as himself. They, like he, would want to use water, and would rightly blame those who disregarded the ban. Hume's account is to be preferred to Kant's precisely because, instead of depending on the abstract reasoning powers of an individual – which, like a kind of mathematics, could be entirely hypothetical and remain valid even if no actual other people existed – it invokes the idea of other real human beings in the same predicament as oneself, with whom therefore one can sympathise and so cooperate.

There are other animals that are social animals, but we are unique in knowing that this is what we are. We are thus able to recognise that the world is often dangerous and hostile, and that though we may try to foresee the consequences of our actions, the future is uncertain, and disaster may strike unexpectedly. Our life is precarious, but we, human beings, can understand that we are all in the same boat and can choose to cooperate with the other passengers to keep the boat from sinking, and must do so for everyone's sake. The more we have learned, over the centuries, about the universe and our place within it, the widerspread has become our potential recognition of the common plight of humanity.

We positively *need* morality to alleviate the predicament that we are all in together. We cannot make things perfect (though we can have visions of perfection) but we can at least determine not to make things worse. This, it seems to me, is the basis of our admiration for the human virtues of courage, honour, truthfulness, loyalty and above all, love, pity, kindliness and whatever is the opposite of arrogance and self-importance. It is imagination that enables us to aspire to a world in which such virtues prevail. And it is our human capacity to recognise such virtues that is the foundation of morality. There could be no morality without the acceptance, as fact, that human beings are capable, as all animals are, of causing each other great harm, and, moreover, that they are frequently tempted to do so in their own immediate interest, or for some other destructive cause. Thus the resistance to temptation is at the heart of individual morality.

It was Auguste Comte (1798–1857), that undoubtedly dotty but highly influential philosopher, who first insisted that morality depended on man's natural ability to consider the good, not only of '*moi*', but of '*autrui*'. It was he who coined the word 'altruism' (from the Italian '*altrui*' meaning 'someone else') and insisted that morality arose out of this natural ability, combined with increasing understanding of actual society ('sociology', his other linguistic coinage) The idea of God, bestowing rewards for good behaviour and punishments for bad, was not only unnecessary to morality, but positively inimical to it, insofar as it suggested that people might aim to behave morally well for selfish reasons.

Comte doubtless exaggerated the extent to which religious people are in fact motivated by the thought of rewards and punishments. And certainly this motivation for morally good behaviour was denied from the early stages of Christianity ('My God, I love thee not because/I hope for heaven thereby/Nor yet because who love thee not/Are lost eternally', as the Lenten hymn has it); yet it could not be denied that those whose morality derived from Christianity, and who were obedient to Christian principles, at least knew that in some sense they were on the winning side, for this was God's promise. Those whose morality was purely human in its foundation could have no such assurance. They could only do their best, in the world as they found it, hoping to do more good than harm, with no comforting assurance of success.

Comte lessened the impact of his arguments by his plan to found a new religion out of his Humanism, complete with saints and liturgy; a religion built on Roman Catholicism, without its essential ingredient, God. It would be hard to imagine a more hopeless plan: religion is of slow growth, and requires tradition and continuity, the sense of antiquity, indeed of eternity. Such things cannot be created by fiat. But in themselves his arguments seem to me of profound importance.

Morality arises out of community, cooperation and love. There can be no morality except in a social context; that is, a context involving other people. Even if a man marooned on a desert island set moral rules for himself, he would be only pretending that he lived in society. The idea of other people would be in his mind; he would have learned morality in the days before his exile. Such a view of the origin of ethics begins to look close to the theories of John Milbank and other radically orthodox Christians whom I discussed above (pp. 99–104). In fact there are two crucial differences. In the first place, to say that morality begins and ends in sympathy and cooperation within society is to speak of the essence of morality, not of its day-to-day manifestation. Practical action within small communities is not necessarily the only or the best form of morals and politics. Second, Radical Orthodoxy hold that there can be no stability, no certainty, in moral principles unless they come from an unchanging, non-human, non-natural Being, without whose commands moral judgements are no more reliable than fashion or whim. Lucretius observed that it was fear that created the gods. It was the fear of inexplicable natural disasters and unpredictable chances that drove earlier people to religious observance. For the new Christian socialists it is the fear of social anarchy. They seek an everlasting cement to bind society together. Christianity provides this cement, because it preaches that God is not only outside the world, everlasting and immovable, but also in it, God to be seen in man, among whom Christians must work. The Positivist view (to name it after Comte and his adherents) sees that morality is not required to be absolute or fixed. It may change, and has changed, over time (as, for example, moral attitudes to women have changed since the first Christian era); what remains constant is human need, and human engagement with the needs of others than ourselves. Of course it is possible to conceive of a terrible time when no one on earth was thus engaged, when no one cared about anybody else, and no one wanted to do good rather than harm, or be virtuous rather than vicious. This would be the anarchy that is rightly dreaded. It is the outcome that any human being who can envisage it most wants to avoid. But it is a fact about human

First, however, there are two general points. We must remember that religion is not all of one kind. I do not mean that there are different faiths; that is a fact we are not likely to forget. But there are different degrees or levels of belief with which any religion is embraced. In a speech in the House of Lords during the debate on one of Lord Joffe's euthanasia Bills, from which I have already quoted (see pp. 45–46), Baroness Richardson of Calow referred to those Christians who had hitherto relied on the security of the proposition that death is in the hands of God, whereas in fact the responsibility of bringing about death had largely passed into human hands. Such believers are often guilty, she implied, of shuffling off the burden of thinking about their human duty to other people and using God as an excuse to make such burdensome thought unnecessary. I do not deny, and I am certain that Baroness Richardson would not deny, that there are religious believers who in all honesty believe that there exists a benevolent God who gives life to individual human beings, cares for them while they are alive, and takes away their life in His own good time, to replace it with life everlasting. And they believe this, or think that they do so, in the same way as they believe that sugar is soluble or that snow is white. They do not feel the need to argue about it. But at the same time there are many people who would answer affirmatively the question whether they believe that God exists, but would go on, if pressed, to admit that this belief is only a vague part of their system of beliefs; or that belief in God is different from empirical beliefs about the natural world. And of even the more positive believers, we may raise the question what their 'belief' actually entails. For they will also speak of their faith, even their unshakeable faith; but faith, as everyone knows, is different from belief. If we like our coffee sweet, and put sugar in it, we do not need faith that it will dissolve; we know, or believe unshakeably, that it will, provided it was really sugar that was in the spoon. We can show that sugar is soluble, by demonstrating with our coffee. Our daily practical life is based upon a collection of such beliefs. In contrast, even those who claim to have had dramatic personal religious experiences, in which they have encountered God, cannot actually show that it was God they encountered. Thus Sartre used the story of Abraham, commanded by God to sacrifice Isaac, not to prove the existence of God, but to prove that we are responsible for all our actions. For it was Abraham himself who chose to identify the commanding voice as that of God.

The second general point is even more obvious: we are, most of us, even today, capable of holding contradictory beliefs at the same time. We are not always, or often, clear-headed. But we have probably become rather more clear-headed than we were before the Age of Enlightenment, or before Darwin. Writing about pre-Reformation religion, Patrick Collinson (*The Oxford Illustrated History of Christianity*, edited by John McManners, Oxford University Press, 1990, chapter 7) reminds us that Luther's prince, the Elector of Saxony, Frederick the Wise, was not only the patron of a modern university, with a progressive department of theology, but at the same time the owner of a collection of relics with the supposed potency to reduce by thousands of years the time that dead souls would have to spend in purgatory. The collection, like a modern library, was looked after by curators and there was a printed catalogue. It is hard to imagine the role of religion in fifteenth-century Europe. So when I try to analyse the nature of religion, and ask whether it has a role in politics, it is the twenty-first century that I am talking about, and no other.

Let us concede, at any rate, that, today, religious belief is not ordinary belief, and let us ask whether, therefore, the concept of God is not sometimes illegitimately, dishonestly, used by those who want ballast for their moral beliefs, or who shy away from thinking of the specifically moral implications of the issues before them. By this I mean the implications for what we owe to those other people who are in the same boat as ourselves, and whose well-being we are morally bound to consider as equal to or more important than our own. The tendency of religious parliamentarians to abandon their religious objections to a proposal, after a single reference, for example, to the sanctity of life, and to move on to the consequences of the measure in the empirical world (a tendency, as I have suggested, that may partly arise from a desire to seem reasonable and open to argument) is sometimes matched by a tendency to fall back on a reference to God's supernatural plan, to avoid discussion of the consequences of a proposed change in the world we inhabit. God, being admittedly mysterious, may sometimes be used as a block to prevent further argument. And this is a less than honest use of religion, at least in a parliamentary or political context. One of the worst features of the pronouncements of George W. Bush was his tendency to justify his actions in the name of an undiscussed religious faith, supposed automatically both to allow him to occupy the moral high ground and to prevent challenge. One of the most disgraceful refusals to think consequentially, in terms of a moral policy, is the refusal of the Roman Catholic Church to recognise the effect that the use of contraceptives might have on the spread of AIDS in Africa.

However, to notice that there are different kinds of religious faith, and different degrees of belief in our access to the will of God, does not advance us much in trying to establish whether religion is necessary to society. Religion, it hardly needs to be said, is a construct, like morality itself, of the human imagination. Plainly, if there had been no human beings on earth, no one to raise questions about how they came to be there, or how they can save themselves from danger or put up with the inevitability of death, there would have been no religion. There would have been no one to think of it. Religion, again like morality, arises from the position that human beings find that they occupy in the world, their sense that they are not wholly in control of what happens to them, that there is much all around them that is mysterious, that they need some defence against what they suffer, whether at the hands of other people or from the disasters that nature itself may cause. Gods are the embodiment of the mysterious and the unpredictable. Libations and sacrifices may cause them to be merciful or to give up their mischief, and so give back to people some control over their lives, through the medium of priests and prophets, who can interpret the signs of the gods' pleasure or displeasure. The gods, if placated, may even be helpful to human enterprise (though not often in a very active way. The frequently reproduced Attic black-figure vase depicting Heracles holding up the world, with the goddess Athena standing by, hand lifted to assist, but not actually making contact with the great burden, seems typical of the relationship between gods and humankind.)

The practice of religious observance as a way of either placating the gods or ascertaining their intentions may long outlive any literal belief in the gods themselves, like the habit that many retain of touching wood if they express some cherished hope, or carefully avoiding walking under ladders (though there may be good prudential reasons for this as well). Readers of Robert Harris's *Lustrum* (Hutchinson, 2009) will recall that Cicero at one time held the office of Augur, the chief priest in the Roman republic, one of whose tasks it was to consult the entrails of a chicken before a meeting of the Senate to see whether the gods were favourable or unfavourable to the meeting. It was possible for the Augur to postpone a meeting almost indefinitely, for political reasons, by declaring the augury unfavourable. Referring to this practice, Gilbert Murray, in a collection of essays published in his old age (Gilbert Murray, *Stoic, Christian and Humanist*, George Allen and Unwin, 1940, p. 181), wrote:

'[Cicero] considered it of the utmost importance that the Roman people should continue to observe the traditional pieties and sanctities of the Roman religion; he duly performed the rites and took the auspices. Yet ... he quotes with approval Cato's expression of wonder that two haruspices [priests] can look each other in the face without laughing. The priests of the modern Roman Church when presiding over certain miracles in the South of Italy may well feel the same difficulty as the haruspices did, and no doubt surmount it as successfully.'

Murray goes on to quote from Gibbon, who attributed to the educated classes of ancient Rome the view that to the uneducated all religions were equally true, to philosophers equally false, and to statesmen equally useful. Cicero's position, though understandable, perhaps necessary as well as useful, seems a plain case of dishonesty in matters of religion, not unlike that of those who use God to hoist them onto the moral high ground, but perhaps even more disingenuous. Are we, historically, in the same sort of position as Cicero, using religion when it suits us, politically, but otherwise regarding it as outworn superstition, suitable only for the uneducated?

I do not think that this does justice to the role of religion in society today, largely because of the imaginative and cohesive power of the monotheistic religions. Long before Cicero was struggling with his intellectual conscience, a huge change in religious sensibility had come about through the story of Moses, who was commanded by God to lead the Israelites out of their bondage in Egypt (historically perhaps as early as the thirteenth century BC), and who was then led by God into darkness at the top of Mount Sinai, where he was given the Torah, the teaching, to hand it on in turn to the Israelites. This story, told in the Book of Exodus, is the foundation of the Christian tradition with which I am especially concerned. The Torah contained, among many rules and regulations, the Ten Commandments, still part of the Christian as well as the Jewish tradition, and these commandments were held to be the revealed source of all morality, at least until Jesus gave his commands. There could be no better illustra-

tion than the story of Moses of how the moral needs of a belea-
guered and closed society were authoritatively met. The authority
came from the origin of the laws in God's direct encounter with
Moses. The laws that Moses was given on Mount Sinai, on tablets
of stone, were the biblical counterparts of the supernatural laws
of God or of Nature – standing above the positive law and justifying it – which Blackstone (and Antigone) so firmly believed in
and Bentham so deeply ridiculed.

With Moses, then, God became one God, He became the
source of morality and there was none other to be worshipped.
He was not merely the superior among the gods, like Zeus, who
after all, like all the other gods, had a mother and a father and
was not the creator of the world, and who, moreover, by human
standards, did not always behave very well. The one God, by contrast, was both all-powerful and the very origin of human goodness, and had existed for all eternity, the same.

The concept of this God found its most eloquent written expression in the Psalms, most of which are thought to date from
after the exile of the people of Judah in Babylon (c. 597–538 BC),
and in the work of Deutero-Isaiah, probably around the same
time in the sixth century BC. The latter wrote of God:

'Who hath measured the waters in the hollow of his hand, and meted
out heaven with the span, and comprehended the dust of the earth in a
measure and weighed the mountains in scales, and the hills in a balance?
… And Lebanon is not sufficient to burn, nor the beasts thereof sufficient for a burnt offering. All nations before him are as nothing; and
they are counted to him less than nothing and vanity.' (Isaiah 40:12,
16–17)

This God, Deutero-Isaiah tells us, made the world, and is worthy
of infinite awe and worship on account of his limitless power, his
eternity, and his eternal and unchanging laws, while burnt offer-
ings and sacrifices are of little interest to him. By the time of this
prophet, the one God has taken to himself all the mystery and

majesty of nature, as well as all the moral authority of the law. Then, five or six centuries later, when the Emperor Augustus was still able to declare himself a god, came the Messiah, long-awaited in Jewish tradition, but acknowledged as such only by a few rebel Jews. And Christianity eventually broke away from the rest of Judaism. In time, the doctrine of the Holy Trinity was formulated – linking the supernatural to the natural, the divine to the human.

Among the lists of rules contained in the first five books of the Old Testament, the Pentateuch, there are also stories; and these form part of Jewish historical and mythological tradition, binding the community together, along with the moral and social rules. Such traditional stories were essential to the religion itself. They gave insight into the will of God, and authority to the moral laws. The authority derives from the sense that this morality has its own continuity, and is therefore not about to fall victim to arbitrary change; it is rooted in history. This is why orthodox Jews are scrupulous about the rules to this day, fearing the power of liberalisation and insisting, if not on the historical accuracy of the scriptures, then at least on the divine origin of the regulations, their status as revealed. However, it is not only within the confines of orthodox Judaism that stories play a crucial part in religion.

In all religions, including that of the Greeks and Romans, there have been defining stories or myths. Indeed many people think of ancient classical religions as consisting of nothing but myth. That is certainly a mistake: rituals such as the various initiation ceremonies, often obscurely referred to in Greek literature as the Mysteries, and the sorts of ceremonies carried out by the Roman Augurs were more important aspects of religion than the mythology. Nevertheless, the rituals and ceremonies of religion are founded on the stories that explain them, just as the ritual of Holy Communion in the Christian Church is founded on the story of the Last Supper.

In the twentieth century much Christian theology was concerned with the concept of myth and the extent to which the scriptures could be understood as myth. The theologian Paul Tillich (1886–1965) was a leader in this movement. He argued that myth could show truth, but that one should constantly look critically at biblical myths, abandoning those whose meaning seems to have deserted them, interpreting and reinterpreting those which still had a living force. Rather confusingly, this process was known as 'demythologising the Bible', a term coined by another theologian of German origin, Rudolf Bultmann (1884–1976). Such a programme was, of course, wholly rejected by those whose Christianity depended on their belief that the Bible was, in its entirety, and regardless of its history, revealed truth; yet Tillich and those who thought like him were undoubtedly influential. Along with those theologians who from the nineteenth century onwards had treated the Bible essentially historically, he made the fundamentalist standpoint patently untenable, as it is for the most part today. It would now be generally agreed that to treat the Bible as a kind of once-and-for-all revelation, with no regard either to its historical context or its variable truth-content, is a view to be embraced only by cranks and fanatics. But one must ask, what are the consequences for the moral authority of religion of holding the stories of the Bible to be myths?

I remember in the 1970s going to a series of seminars entitled 'Myth', attended entirely, apart from myself, by theologians (and I went because I was interested in imagination and narrative at the time). It was presided over by a highly intelligent canon of Christ Church and professor of theology, Maurice Wiles, and it was concerned with the relationship between truth and mythology. Earlier than this, J. R. R. Tolkien had described his own epic, *The Lord of the Rings*, as not just an adventure story about an invented race, but as a True Myth. He was convinced that the more he built into the book, and the more consistent geography and even linguistics it contained, the more truth it could reveal, becoming a coherent, free-standing whole. The concept of true myth, then, was at the centre of our discussion. The trouble was, however, that though it was easy for us to agree that the story of the Garden of Eden was in every sense a myth, and many stories of miracles even in the New Testament were myths, there was little else we could agree on.

The Garden of Eden, of course, was a perfect case of mythology. In the first place, it was linked to the story of the creation of the world, and that had always, since ancient times and in all religions, been a proper subject of mythology. For the myths of creation told an explanatory story about that for which no scientific explanation could be found. The story of the Garden of Eden was, however, not a primitive attempt at a scientific hypothesis; it was not a less well-informed version of the Big Bang. It deeply appealed to the imagination because it was used to explain the human as well as the physical aspect of the universe, the beginning of disobedience and shame, those essentially moral features of the human world. Moreover, it had the other great property of myth, it could be told again and again with new interpretations, like the story of Oedipus. One has only to think of the angel retelling the story in Milton's *Paradise Lost*. The concept of a paradise lost is, in any case, a recurring and an archetypical theme, especially in Romantic poetry. So we were on safe ground with the Garden of Eden. None of us had any doubt that here we were dealing with myth, fruitful, lasting and appealing to some human need, both explanatory and emotional.

But there were some stories which it seemed that this group of theologians could not deem to be myth; some accounts which, if they were to continue to call themselves Christians (which they really had to, all of them being professionals, academics, chaplains, cathedral clergy), they must claim to believe as literal truth.

Among these, the most prominent was the story of the Resurrection of Jesus (they were, as I remember, prepared to let go the Virgin Birth). When we came to the Resurrection, we came to a full stop. We were not allowed to treat it as myth. The crucifixion was taken to be a datable historical fact, whatever its significance. It was hoped that the Resurrection could be the same. (But it should perhaps be noted that as long before as 1947 the then Bishop of Birmingham, Ernest Barnes, had published a book called *The Rise of Christianity*, in which he accorded the status of myth not only to the Virgin Birth and the Miracles, but also to the Resurrection. He was deemed unfit for episcopal office by the Archbishop of Canterbury (or, at least, was told that he should consider his position). But he did not resign.

It is easy to understand the reluctance of any Christian to put the story of the Resurrection into the category of myth; what then would be left of Christian doctrine? Richard Holloway takes it to be a central myth of Christianity, a story symbolic of the possibility of many resurgences and renewals, and important because of its vast effect on history. Its effect has been fact, whether it was fact or not. Yet he recognises that in treating it so he is perhaps putting himself beyond the bounds of Christianity (see Richard Holloway, *Doubts and Loves*, Canongate, 2001, pp.139–140). But, in any case, the word 'myth' is deeply ambiguous. It is generally held to be at least in part what I have already suggested – an explanation for something which science has not yet reached to explain. But this carries with it the implication that myths are essentially meant to be rejected, as soon as science has caught up. From this derives the common use of the word to mean 'a superstition', 'an old wives' tale' or a 'baseless false belief, held only by the ignorant'. So to speak of the stories on which a religion is founded as myths implies, at the very least, that there is a distinction to be drawn between the sophisticated and the simple-minded. A reading from the scriptures would be understood completely differently by the ignorant and the learned, or those in the know. And this has the further implication that, like Cicero reading the signs, the more intelligent clergy are somehow deceiving their congregations, allowing them to suppose that they believe something that they do not believe, an uncomfortable position for them to accept. It is akin to the position of those parents who perpetuate the myth of Father Christmas. One day the truth will come out. So, carrying this sort of connotation, the word 'myth' seems less than helpful in talking about religion, except in the context of long-abandoned religions, which cannot any longer lay claim to believers. The concept of a 'true myth' is too paradoxical to be illuminating. We need a less value-laden word to refer to the form in which the origin of the world, and the origin of morality, are presented to us in the great religions.

All of the great monotheistic religions are presented in their scriptures at least partly in narrative. Even the writings of St Paul – an integral figure in the growth of the early Church and of Christianity itself – starts with the narrative of the events on the road to Damascus, and continues with his travels; and even the Book of Revelation is the narrative of a dream. So the word 'narrative' might be a more useful word by which to refer to what lies at the heart of religion. Moreover, a narrative is neutral between the true and the false. A narrative may be either fictional or historical; it may set out to tell what really happened, give an interpretation or version of what happened, or refer to something imagined or invented. But 'narrative' is often used adjectivally, meaning a particular style. And I am looking for a word that refers not to the style of telling but exclusively to what it is that is told, the content. And for this the word 'story', wider in meaning than 'myth' and less value-laden, is possibly the best (though of course it is true that in a rather old-fashioned sense a story can also mean a false story. In my childhood, the nursery maid used to accuse me of telling stories, if she thought I was lying.) I shall therefore abandon the concept of 'demythologising', and consider only the relation between religion and stories, and the connection of both with truth.

C. S. Lewis, the Christian convert, popular war-time religious broadcaster, novelist, and above all scholarly and perceptive critic, contributed an essay, 'On Story', to a volume of essays presented to Charles Williams and published in the 1950s (*Essays Presented to Charles Williams*, William B. Eerdmans Publishing Co., Grand Rapids, Mich., 1966). Writing, not about great literature but about what may be thought of as pure, basic stories, stories for children, he suggested that the story of Jack the Giant Killer, for example, appeals to the imagination because it embodies a familiar emotion, common to all human beings (and certainly to all children), in this case fear, and fear directed towards a certain kind of object. He is right, it seems to me, to suggest that emotions that are directed towards an object, such as fear or jealousy, love or awe, cannot be described or conveyed except by reference to their proper object. How else could one distinguish between anxiety, directed towards the thought of what someone may be suffering, and jealousy, concerned with the thought of what they may be up to? It is by reason of the nature of the object that we can give a name to the emotion. In the case of the children's story, the peculiar sort of fear embodied in the story of Jack is the fear of the gigantic; its slowness, its heaviness, its monstrosity and unpredictability. 'Nature', Lewis says, 'has that in her which compels us to invent giants, and only giants will do.' The whole quality of the response to this story is determined by the fact that it is giants against whom Jack is pitted. The test, according to Lewis, of whether the child's imagination has been touched by the idea in the story is how often they want to return to it, have it told or read to them again, and re-experience its central point. The tension of anticipation, of wanting to know what happens next as the story unfolds for the first time, in its successive episodes, is not the same as the imaginative revelation that comes with repetition. 'Not until the curiosity, the sheer narrative lust has been given its sop and laid to sleep are we at leisure to savour the real beauties ... till then it is like wasting a great wine on a ravenous natural thirst.' Surprise, paradox, denouement in a plot, are all better understood when we know what is coming next. It is the 'irony' at the heart of both tragedy and comedy. The purpose of a story, says Lewis, is to try to catch an idea, and to convey it in terms of the concrete, the temporal and the transitory. 'In art and in life, both', he said, 'we are always trying to catch in our net of successive moments something that is not successive.' It is, I would argue, imagination that reaches the story, that interprets it so that its successive moments yield up what truth it may contain. This it seems to me is as accurate a description of our reading of the Gospels as of Jack the Giant Killer, or indeed of the novels of Tolstoy or of Proust. The question 'Did it really happen?' drops out as irrelevant. And indeed, as with Proust's novel and as with the Gospels, it would often be a question very difficult to answer. *Something* happened, and was transformed into a story.

What I am suggesting is that we often read stories, whether we identify them as history or as fiction, or as historical fiction, in search of something we can identify as truth; not the whole truth but at least a truth. Of course we may look for entertainment or amusement as well; and there are those who are entertained by accounts of fantastic or apparently totally random occurrences., or stories of people whose motivation is, by normal standards, unintelligible, but if a story or a novel is too outlandish, seems too far from any possible reality, or is not held together by anything that makes sense to us from our own experience, then I for one tend to reject it. (This explains why I have never been able to get either pleasure or insight from Iris Murdoch's novels.) Our imagination has nothing to feed on in such cases.

This implies a kind of realism; it suggests that we can distinguish what is true and meaningful, what is true *of* something, from what has no relation to reality. This realism is totally repudiated by the critical methods of postmodernism, whether applied to literature or to the texts of religion. The central tenet of postmodernism is that there is no such thing as truth: that the supposition that language may in any way correspond to or mirror reality is simply an illusion. It is another, though doubtless more sophisticated, illusion to suppose that language can *hint at* or *suggest* a truth. For there is no such thing as a truth that is separate from language or a truth that language aims to disclose. There are some postmodernist theologians who think of the Gospels as stories, certainly, but who would not claim that they were either literally true or that they aimed to catch in their net something that we might accept or experience as true. On such a view as theirs, we cannot get outside language. We may fancy that there is a non-linguistic, non-temporal reality to which we aspire, but there cannot be. For when we speak of such a reality we are still trapped in the language of the everyday world. The American philosopher, Richard Rorty, the guru of postmodernism, was much influenced by his study of the work of Jacques Derrida, who held that it is futile to ask whether a 'text' (that is images, or words, spoken or written), is true because there is nothing in the world that the text represents. The text itself is just another thing in the world, and can be interpreted in any way that anyone likes. Such interpretation is 'play', and perfectly free, carrying its own validity (Jacques Derrida, *Speech and Phenomena*, Northwestern University Press, 1973) (I freely confess that what I have just written makes no sense whatsoever. But it is Derrida's idea of 'play': that everything should be unintelligible, written in his own sort of nonsense-language.) Rorty also relied on Wittgenstein's supposed view of philosophy, according to which philosophical questions are indicative of intellectual discomforts that can be relieved by understanding how language works, and how we use it in practice. Language does not reflect a separate non-linguistic world but is a self-sufficient series of conventions by which we live in society, a necessary tool that we have built up for communicating, its meaning exemplified in its use. According to Rorty, then, we should not think of philosophers or theologians, or indeed story-tellers, as seeking truth (about anything) but as simply inhabitants of the only world that exists, telling each other tales the purpose of which is simply to keep the conversation going. These stories will constantly change, and so will the interpretation of them. But they do not strive after anything beyond themselves (see Richard Rorty, *Philosophy and the Mirror of Nature*, Blackwell, 1980).

Such a theory is related not only to Wittgenstein's beliefs about the function of language, but to theories originating in the visual arts. In the second half of the twentieth century it was frequently asserted that there was no single privileged point of view from which an object could be seen, or represented, but that every object had innumerable facets that present themselves to different viewers. For example, it was argued that to teach people the rules of perspective when teaching them to draw was the result of a kind of imperialism, one view having taken precedence over and suppressed all other equally 'valid' views. This kind of postmodernism was much loved by radical feminists, who argued that there was a woman's angle from which even such subjects as mathematics and philosophy, physics and biology, might legitimately be approached. The postmodernist idea that there are different games that we can play with language, once we learn the rules, carries with it the same kind of radical relativism that is implied by the claim that there is an infinite number of equally 'valid' ways of seeing the world or interpreting it: there is no one final right way, the truthful way.

In the spirit of postmodernism, the Cambridge theologian Don Cupitt held that by the 1990s the idea that a story could somehow encapsulate a truth that was separate from itself had already been abandoned. No one, he implied, could any longer embrace such an idea. He therefore distinguishes his new account of what a story is from what he calls 'the standard answer' to the question of how the temporal and changing can reflect truth, which is permanent and unchanging; This question, he says, is as old as Western philosophy.

'The standard answer went like this [and it will be recognised that this is a version of C. S. Lewis's answer]: the temporal successiveness of the story, in the reading or the telling of it, cannot be the vehicle of truth. But the story completed, like a finished painting, may be able to function as an allegory of timeless truth. The finished story as an icon, set-piece or tableau is not quite itself the truth but it can serve as a symbol of the truth ... And if the truth signified is thus something quite distinct from the sign that signifies it, then the sign as such is only instrumental. It is not itself the holy thing. So you may have a good deal of freedom to retell the story or to embroider it, if thereby you can better bring out the unchanging non-narrative truth that the story is trying to point to ... The Real Truth signified, the truth you dared not touch, was not located within the movement of the mere signs. It was outside the text, and the text only bore witness to it.'

And he goes on:

'When, however, as has happened with us, truth fully returns into time, narrative and the movement of language, the interpreter's task begins to look very different ... Truth is no longer something self-identical unchanging and subsisting outside the text, but is inherent in the very motion of the signs that compose the text. Truth is no longer something out there: it is a way of words. The preacher, interpreter or artist is now making truth in the telling of the tale. Truth is no longer held firm and self-identical in eternity; instead, it lives and grows and changes in time.' (Don Cupitt, *What is a Story?*, SCM Press, 1991, p. 23)

His rather gloomy rhetoric ends with these words: 'story structures time and the world and keeps darkness and death at bay, at

141

least for a while. We are listening to Scheherazade again, putting off death by listening to tales through the night. Narrative, only narrative conquers dark and the void' (*ibid.*, p. 80).

Cupitt regards the history of theology as a perpetual and necessarily unsuccessful attempt to climb out from the language through which we deal with and describe and negotiate the world of human beings and other natural objects, into a separate and more elevated world. This brings him to a view of religion (distinct from theology) as a practical activity, to be engaged in when we realise that we are never going to get to a timeless truth, or a master-narrative. He could have quoted Wordsworth:

' 'Tis a thing impossible, to frame
Conceptions equal to the soul's desires …'

(Wordsworth, *The Excursion*, Book IV, l. 136).

And the sooner we, and theologians realise this the better. But, according to Cupitt, each time we fail, and come back to earth, we may become better at reconciling ourselves to the fact that this is all there is. And so we may at last give up the search for God, and concentrate on man, beginning to 'love the unloveable'. Richard Holloway (*op. cit.*, pp. 38–41) quotes from W. B. Yeats's poem 'The Second Coming' to illustrate the same earth-bound view:

'Now that my ladder's gone
I must lie down where all the ladders start
In the foul rag and bone shop of the heart.'

There are no ladders left. Such a view of religion seems at first sight not unlike that of John Milbank and his Radical Orthodoxy. The crucial difference is that the idea of God outside the world and setting standards to which we can aspire has dropped out. It is greatly to Don Cupitt's moral credit that, coming back to earth, he believes that there are some stories that are nicer than others; that it is preferable to love people than to eliminate them. But what he comes back to is, it seems to me, a morality derived from the world, a humanism, not a religion; and it is hard to see how he could disagree.

It is not theologians alone who engage in the arguably fruitless enterprise of seeking the permanent in the shifting, the truth that somehow exists beneath the surface or above the mundane. It is the enterprise of anyone, interested in religion or not, who is concerned with what are often vaguely called 'Spiritual Values'. This is not a particularly enlightening term, and is avoided as far as possible by many people, including myself. It is especially suspect to those who are positively hostile to religion, and who aim, for example, for education to be totally secularised and hold that church or other 'faith schools' should be abolished. For they rightly think that many people identify the spiritual with the religious, and that when the spiritual is introduced as a necessary element in the school curriculum, and spiritual values are identified as among those that education will foster, it is religion that is surreptitiously being introduced as part of what is to be taught. Similarly, when the Hospice Movement was founded, to care for terminally ill cancer patients, much was made of its meeting not just the physical needs of patients but their emotional and 'spiritual' needs as well; and it was suspect in some quarters, on the ground that, its founder being a devout Christian, Christianity had undue influence within the hospices, and was, it was alleged, sometimes forced on patients who rejected the whole idea of God in any form.

Nevertheless, though to some extent I share these suspicions, some word seems to be needed to encompass that aspect of the human imagination which has immortal longings. Because they possess imagination, human beings may feel deeply, if only occasionally, that through the immediate and the concrete they have glimpses of something else. It is only human beings, among all living animals, who as far as we know, have, or imagine that they have, these glimpses; and Don Cupitt is right to think that if religion is the futile aspiration to reach the timeless through the temporal telling of the story, this is logically connected with the human possession of language, without which there would manifestly be no stories. I am content to refer to the human imagination as the spirit of man, and ascribe to the human spirit the birth of morality and of law; and further to acknowledge it as the creator not only of religion, but of all our aesthetic reaction to nature and the arts.

A key concept in this aspect of the imagination is that of the symbol. Indeed Cupitt, as we have seen, speaks of the, as he supposed, outdated view of stories (roughly, the view of C. S. Lewis) as treating the story as a whole, the completed story, as a sign or symbol of something other than itself, the medium through which we seek to apprehend something permanent, a truth. He also refers to stories regarded in this way as allegories. But he has, I think, overlooked an important distinction here. Coleridge, in Appendix B of the *Statesman's Manual*, distinguished between allegory and symbol in the following way:

'Now an allegory is nothing but a translation of abstract notions into picture language, which is itself nothing but an abstraction from objects of the senses. On the other hand a Symbol is characterised by a translucence of the special in the individual, of the general in the special, of the universal in the general: above all by the translucence of the eternal through the temporal.'

An allegory, that is to say, is a story we think up *in order to* illustrate an idea in concrete terms: a symbol is something existing before our eyes or ears, which, not being invented for this purpose, nevertheless means, or seems to mean, something other than itself. With allegory, the idea comes first, clearly formulated, and deliberately illustrated in the story. With symbols, it is the thing, the object in the world (whether part of a story or not) that speaks to us of something else, of an idea that we may not be able to formulate, but which we possess only through the reaction we have to the object before us, that which we treat as a symbol. Coleridge, who as a young man was perpetually searching for meanings in the objects of sense, and who was an appreciative, though a sometimes confused, reader of Kant's Critiques, suggested that what the symbol speaks to us of must remain mysterious. The Understanding gives us knowledge, but only of things we experience. It works, in a roughly Kantian sense, to organise experience and regularise the world as it appears to us, in certain fixed categories, so that we can pronounce one thing to be the cause of another, or one substance different from another. But what Kant called the Ideas of Reason, distinct from the categories of the Understanding, could never be material for this classificatory or organising faculty. In a conversation that took place in 1811, and was later published by his nephew, Henry (H. C. Coleridge, *Table Talk*, 1838), Coleridge complained (in true Old Bore's style, we may think) that no one any longer had any reverence for anything; and he explained that this was because people 'had conceptions only'.

'As conception is the work of the mere understanding, and as all that is conceived may be comprehended, it is impossible that a man should reverence that, to which he always feels something in himself superior. If it were possible to conceive God in a strict sense, that is as we conceive a horse or a tree, even God himself could not excite any reverence, though he might excite fear or terror ... But reverence which is the synthesis of love and fear, is only due from man, indeed is only excitable in man, towards ideal truths which are always mysteries to the understanding.'

The idea of the symbolic is central to the religious imagination. Religion apart, the proneness of human beings to treat objects in the world as symbolic is a chief function of imagination, as important to it as the ability to think about the past and the possible future, another way of contemplating 'what is not'. For the symbol is both itself, and something that it stands for but is *not* before our eyes; in Coleridge's words, it is translucent. Kant argued that all that we claim to believe about God must be expressed in symbolic language. To think otherwise would be to fall into anthropomorphism, forming God in our own image. To claim to know the nature of God, even that he exists, is to mistake the nature of human knowledge, which, as Coleridge learned from his reading of Kant, must be a matter of applying the categories of the understanding to the raw material supplied by our senses, our experience of how the world appears to us. Kant held that there is no such thing as metaphysical knowledge; knowledge is of the physical world, and of that alone. But since we are aware of the physical world by our senses, that physical world is a world of appearances. The three great Ideas of Reason, namely God, Freedom and Immortality, are not parts of knowledge, but are necessary to our thought. We cannot know them to be true, but they are assumptions for all our thinking. Knowledge is of the world as it appears to us. But if there is an appearance, according to Kant, there must be something of which it is an appearance, a thing in-itself. We can think this but we can never perceive such a thing. Thus, for example, the Idea of Freedom is used by us in our assumption that we *can* do whatever it is that the categorical imperative rationally dictates we ought to do. But Freedom is not something we can perceive in the world, which is the world of law-governed deterministic science. Things in themselves are 'noumena', thought of, but not grasped or understood.

In the third Critique, *The Critique of Judgment*, Kant – having, as he believed, established in the preceding Critiques objective standards of knowledge and of right action – sets out to explore our subjective methods of engaging with the world, and our subjective reactions to it. He does this through the notion of purpose, which he uses to define the way in which we think of the natural world, when we seek to understand it. We think of it, he argues, *as if* it had a purpose or was controlled by a guiding hand. We need not follow him down these paths. But he uses the same concept – that of purpose or design – to explain what happens when we deem something to be beautiful. For we judge something beautiful when we can discern in it a pattern or a 'point', which is like discerning the purpose of something, what it is for, but which is in fact distinct from any actual or practical purpose. Thus, in hearing a beautiful melody, we may have a sense that it has to end with the very cadence with which it does end. It was, as it were, destined inevitably, designed, to do so. And it is this sense of recognition of pattern that gives us pleasure. But Kant goes on to draw a distinction – a fashionable critical distinction of his time, borrowed from English and Scottish aestheticians such as Addison, Burke and Blair – between the beautiful and the sublime. 'We observe', he says

'that whereas natural beauty conveys a purposiveness in its form, making the object appear as it were pre-adapted to our powers of judgment, so that it thus forms of itself an object of delight, that which … in our apprehension of it excites the feeling of the sublime may appear in point of form to contravene the ends of our powers of judgment, to be ill-adapted to our faculty of presentation and to be as it were an outrage to the imagination, and yet is judged all the more sublime on that account.'

In our apprehension of beauty, that is to say, our ordinary conceptual understanding and our imagination work together; we see the pattern, the regularity, we grasp the shape and the seeming inevitability of a particular curve, a poetic rhythm, or a musical cadence and this is what gives us satisfaction. There is here a sort of order that makes us feel 'that's right', even though we may never have seen or heard the object of our satisfaction before. But with the sublime, our imagination is defeated. We cannot discover any form in what presents itself to us as sublime, or if there is form, it does not exhaust the full content of the object, so that we feel there is always more that eludes our grasp. The sublime, in fact, presents us with another idea, like that of God, Immortality or Freedom, which cannot be wholly articulated. Kant names it an Aesthetic Idea. It may be aspects of nature, towering mountains, great waterfalls, or huge waves breaking against rocks which convey to us the sense of the sublime; or it may be works of art, or literature, or music – works of genius – which give us the same sense of their limitlessness, of their holding for us more than we can express, which we can reach towards but never entirely grasp. Of an Aesthetic Idea, Kant says: 'It is a representation of the imagination which induces much thought yet without the possibility of any definite thought whatever, i.e. concept, being adequate to it, and which language can never get quite on level terms with, or render completely intelligible.' Such a description of an Aesthetic Idea seems to me to fit exactly what might be called Ideas of Religion, through whatever medium they occur, whether through the stories of the Exodus, or the language of the Psalms or, for Christians, the Gospels and symbolism of the Gospel narratives; the birth, crucifixion and resurrection of Jesus; and the celebration of these through the rituals of the church year.

Now the belief that the imagination can lead us through things that are part of the ordinary world to a sense of what lies beyond the world, from the temporal to the timeless, is of course the central and defining idea of Romanticism. Wordsworth described poets thus:

'Like angels stopped upon the wing by sound
Of harmony from Heaven's remotest spheres.
Them the enduring and the transient both
Serve to exalt; they build up greatest things
From least suggestions …'

(Wordsworth, *Prelude*, Book XIV, 198f.)

The Prelude is the story specifically of his imaginative development, through the influence of the mountains and lakes among which he lived as a boy, towards those visionary experiences in which he glimpsed immortality. Coleridge, to whom Wordsworth dedicated *The Prelude*, shared this view of the imagination. There was one moment when he believed that his imagination had deserted him. In 'Dejection: An Ode', he used the word 'joy' for what he believed he had lost for ever, the ability to feel as well as to see the beauty of natural phenomena before his eyes, the stars behind the clouds, the crescent moon, which used to mean something, but at that moment meant nothing:

'I may not hope from outward forms to win
The passion and the life whose fountains are within.'

What he believed he had lost was

'... what nature gave me at my birth,
My shaping spirit of Imagination.'

It was that shaping spirit that enabled him to see meaning in the world beyond what his senses alone could show him. It allowed him to enjoy Aesthetic Ideas, reaching out towards that which language could never encompass.

It is not only poets who experience at least occasionally the sense that they have grasped a truth. Such moments are sometimes referred to as 'epiphanies', and they are occasionally recounted in autobiographies, those real autobiographies, I mean, which attempt to reconstruct what it was actually like to be young, what the quality of one's own life has been (an extraordinarily difficult thing to do). To return briefly to C. S. Lewis: in his autobiography, subtitled 'The Shape of my Early Life' (C. S. Lewis, *Surprised by Joy*, Geoffrey Bles, 1955), he is concerned to recount certain intense experiences that he describes as imaginative experiences in a highly specific sense of that word. Here is one of them

'As I stood beside a flowering currant bush on a summer day there suddenly arose in me without warning, and as if from a depth not of years but of centuries, the memory of that earlier morning, when my brother had brought his toy garden into the nursery. It is difficult to find words strong enough for the sensation which came over me; Milton's "enormous bliss" of Eden (giving the full, ancient meaning to "enormous") comes somewhere near it. It was a sensation, of course, of desire, but desire for what? Not certainly for a biscuit tin filled with moss nor even (though that came into it) for my own past ... and before I knew what I desired, the desire itself was gone, the glimpse withdrawn, the whole world turned commonplace again, or only stirred by a longing for the longing that had just ceased. It had taken only a moment of time; and in a certain sense everything else that had ever happened to me was insignificant in comparison.'

This was an instance of the Romantic imagination at work. For the Romantics, the world seen from behind the eyes of the individual could give rise not only to 'thoughts that do often lie/ Too deep for tears' but to insights, to truths that were felt as absolutely true though incapable of complete linguistic expression, to immortal longings. C. S. Lewis himself, incidentally, made no connection whatsoever between his moments of 'joy', his imaginative epiphanies, and religion, as he later discovered it. Though the description of his conversion to Christianity, described in a later chapter of his autobiography, seems to the reader to have been just such an epiphany, for him it was different in kind, giving rise not to longings for something forever elusive, but to knowledge of solid literal truth. And he admitted that after embracing Christianity as in this sense true he lost interest in his old 'joy', the imaginative experiences of his pre-conversion days.

For the Romantics, individual people hold within themselves the vital clue to the mysterious conjunction of the particular with the universal, the temporal with the timeless. Of course the passion for sensibility, the search after the sublime, whether in nature or in art, led to excesses of the kind so greatly mocked by Jane Austen (and if we want an example of truth contained in stories, we need look no further than her novels). The great visions that came to Wordsworth in the Alps or in his native Cumbria were sometimes sought in Gothic ruins specially constructed in the garden. But the Romantic imagination was firmly entrenched.

When I was still at school, I was given a book by the Cambridge critic F. L. Lucas entitled *The Decline and Fall of the Romantic Ideal*, published in 1937 and long out of print. I valued the book as a quick source of quotations with which to bespatter my essays and bedazzle my teachers (I was careful to conceal my sources). But I did not really take in the message, which was that literature was now politically 'engaged', and that the self-indulgent egocentricity of the Romantic poets, the 'nature lovers', had at last been outgrown. Now, at any rate, I do not believe this to be true. In 2001, the philosopher and critic, Richard Eldridge, published a book with the title *The Persistence of Romanticism: Essays in Philosophy and Literature*, Cambridge University Press, 2001). I believe that Romanticism does and will persist. It seems no more possible to forget the insights of Romanticism than those of Darwinism. And it is the persistence of the Romantic ideal that gives life to religion. Religion is more than a set of moral rules; it is more, even, than doing good in society. It is more than the stories that recount where the moral rules came from, Moses receiving the Torah, Jesus walking in the fields plucking ears of corn on the Sabbath and subverting the rule-governed rigidity of the Jews. It is metaphysical; it depends upon the sense that there is a mystery about the world that we can never quite unravel, that human beings can imaginatively approach this mystery, whether through science or mathematics or other constructions of the imagination, but they will only glimpse the truth. The Romantic ideal opened up the possibility for each finite and short-lived individual to have access, though imperfect and patchy, to something more durable than themselves. It is not a philosophical theory (though Kant played into the hands of such a view); it is a felt response to the world.

The subject-matter of religion is Time and Eternity. Even Christians like those in the Radical Orthodoxy movement, who think of their religion as essentially a matter of action among the poor and the oppressed, see God, or unchangeable goodness, in or through suffering humanity, redemption only in relieving that suffering. This is why the continuity of the great monotheistic religions is so central to them. Anything that the imagination can fasten on as a symbol of endurance, or as signifying a victory over time, will be embraced by religion. This is the role of the Church: not only to hand down tradition but to keep that tradition active in the ceremonies of worship and the liturgy. I can speak, obviously, only for Christianity, but of that religion it is certainly true that there is a sense of awe felt on going into the ancient churches in Europe, and finding worship going on where it went on from the beginnings of Christianity. However different our presuppositions and understandings are from those of worshippers then, a thread can be traced. I was in Russia in the early 1970s, when most churches in Moscow and the then Leningrad had been turned into museums, but there were a few where services might still be held. I and my teenage son were taken to some of these by a teacher, who probably would not have described herself as deeply religious; but the fact that the services were being held, that the Orthodox Church was still living, the liturgy still in use, was moving not only to her but to us (though it must be confessed that the services seemed to involve a very great deal of standing and listening, of which we both, my son and I, became a bit weary). I was never more conscious of the power of the *idea* of continuity and survival, an idea probably even more important to Judaism than to Christianity.

It seems to me that both the Roman Catholic Church and the Church of England have done themselves immeasurable harm by seeking to remove the Romanticism from religion, to remove, that is, the Aesthetic Ideas (in Kant's sense) that it may excite. They have done this by modernising the liturgy and sidelining the King James's Bible, thus removing both tradition and aesthetic pleasure. The Church has become little more than a wealthy charity that holds supporters' meeting which few attend and where a good deal of positive thinking is encouraged by jolly singsongs. And all this has come about in order that people should understand clearly what was always intended to be a mystery, and should take as literally true stories that could never have been more than suggestions of truths that could not be wholly encompassed in language, but whose meaning is for the imagination to interpret. In the House of Lords debate in April 2007, from which I have already quoted, Baroness Rendell of Blabergh, better known as Ruth Rendell, described how she had abandoned her former faith, and lamented the loss of the pleasure she used to get from attending morning service and hearing 'the most beautiful prose ever written in the English language'. Alas, no more. She compared her position with that of Thomas Hardy, 'an atheist, but a "churchy" man, who loved ritual and church music and who said "it is only a sentiment to me now"'. However, it was not the loss of aesthetic pleasure that persuaded her to give up Christianity, but her inability to believe in a benevolent but omnipotent God, and in her support she quoted Darwin who wrote: 'I cannot persuade myself that a beneficent and omnipotent God would have designedly created the Ichneumonidae with the express intention of their feeding within the living bodies of caterpillars'. What he, and she, could not believe was the literal truth of the proposition that God both created the world and is good. What neither he, nor she, could accept in its place was the 'noumenal' or Romantic view of religion, where literal truth is not sought, and within which there may well be no place, even metaphorically, for any such creative God, whether his intents are thought good or bad. The religious imagination, it seems to me, has no need of such a God.

The Church, even the generally liberal and undemanding Church of England, has often been hesitant to acknowledge the centrality to religion of the imagination, the aesthetic, or Hardy's 'sentiment'. Christianity, it would be argued, is not intended to give pleasure, even of an elevated kind, but to teach us how to behave; and in order to learn this we need to acknowledge the truth that God exists and has given us laws that we must obey. To suggest that religion itself comes from the human imagination is to throw away all chance of moral certainty. But I would argue that the concept of morality itself comes from imagination; and the story of the Gospels shows, whatever else, a creative moral imagination at work in Jesus. But, because of its search for the literal and the factually true, the Church has made great efforts, at various times, to eliminate the agreeable or the fanciful from its ceremonies and rituals. Thus as part of the Reformation, with the throwing out of corruption, venality and superstition, church music too had to be cleaned up. There should be no self-indulgent ornamentation, and for each syllable sung there should be no more than one note. Yet however austere their intentions, religious authorities could not do without the arts altogether, and, typically, their attempts to get back or down to basics conspicuously failed. If stained glass was rejected in favour of plain, it turned out that the lightness of the plain glass had a far more uplifting aesthetic effect (we may think of the light in Norwich Cathedral when the sun is shining); if the rule of one syllable/one note is observed, we suddenly have the grandeur and deep authority of the chorale. It is because the Christian believer holds that God's mysteries are in some sense Unspeakable that both architecture and music have been essential to him or her and the Church has never been able to cast them out. (I suppose I must modify what I have just said: there are contemporary fundamentalist Christians who do not think God's mysteries unspeakable. Some of them meet in one another's houses, and 'speak in tongues'.)

The spirit of man, the human imagination, has no expression more astonishing than architecture and music. Goethe opined both that architecture is frozen music, and also that where words end, music begins. I do not subscribe to either of these propositions, the first because as a metaphor I somehow fail to get it, the second because very often, and perhaps especially in the context of religion, it is the combination of music *with* words that has the most powerful effect in all aesthetic experience. The music magnifies and transforms the meaning of the words, whether they are the words set to Schubert's lieder, the words of an operatic libretto, or the sacred words of the mass or the Gospels. One of the most fortunate facts in English history is that when the Church of England broke away from the Roman Catholic Church, and services began to be held in the vernacular, not only was it a time of immense richness and versatility in the English language, but there appeared a crowd of composers, as if magically waiting to compose anthems for the new Church – among them Byrd, Thomas Tomkins, Gibbons, Purcell, Handel. It was not only a religious but a musical revolution. It is impossible to prise apart the music from the words in, say, Purcell's great anthem 'Rejoice in the Lord Alway', or Gibbons's 'This is the Record of John'.

Consider Bach's *St Matthew Passion*. I first heard it just before my seventeenth birthday, in 1941, having been given a ticket and my train fare by my eldest sister – an inspired birthday present. At the Albert Hall I met by chance the mother of a friend of mine, a professional historian of great brilliance, and an atheist. She was apparently as much overwhelmed by the performance as I was, and I wondered then, as I do now, what was the difference between our reactions (I was still at my holy school, and though far from pious, was surrounded by religious observance, both at school and in the cathedral city of Winchester). I have not found an answer to my question. To my ears, among all the glorious and emotion-filled music, there are two settings in that work the genius of which is almost incredible. The first is Peter's denial of

Christ, where the cock crows after his third denial: 'And Peter remembered the word of Jesus, which said unto him, Before the cock crow, thou shalt deny me thrice. And he went out, and wept bitterly.' One does not need a technical knowledge of musical analysis to find Bach's chromatic downward setting of the last phrase almost unbearably moving. Years later I saw a television programme, part of the lamented *South Bank Show*, in which a number of people, none of them, I think, religious, tried to explain their reaction to this and other parts of the *St Matthew Passion*. The actor/producer/psychologist Jonathan Miller, admitting to being unable to hear it without tears, said that the music and the words together portrayed the most awful thing that could happen to a human being, his realisation that he had deliberately betrayed a friend. Of course this is true, but I believe it is only part of the truth. The awfulness for Peter, and what Bach was illuminating, was his, Peter's, and Bach's own, conviction that Jesus was not merely a human friend, but the Son of God. This was the meaning of the story. However sceptical or atheistical one may be, one cannot understand either the story or the music without understanding that this conviction was what the Gospel writer, looking back, was striving to convey. To be moved to tears by this moment in the *Passion* is to exercise historical as well as religious imagination. As R. G. Collingwood argued (*The Idea of History*, Oxford University Press, 1943), the historian must try to think the thoughts of the people he is writing about. The same is true of anyone who reads poetry, or, of course, the Gospels. St Matthew (and the other Synoptic Gospel writers) was trying to make sense of, to make a story out of, what the apostles had earlier experienced, their consciousness of being part of a supernatural intervention in the world. It does not matter whether we think there was such divine intervention. To understand the story, and the music, we must recognise that they thought so. And this is why we may be so much moved by the other moment in the *Passion*: that of the

Centurion 'and they that were with him' who, witnessing the death of Christ, and the earthquake that followed, fearing greatly said: 'Truly this was the Son of God, the Son of God.' The Gospel tells us that even Roman soldiers, not just disciples, on the scene to keep order, could not but share the conviction. And the conviction and amazement are there in the music, the sudden key change, the short intervention of the chorus within the recitative, the repetition, first loud then dying away in astonishment.

In his book about the history of music (based on a hugely enjoyable television series) (*The Big Bangs: The Story of Five Discoveries that Changed Musical History*, Vintage Books, 2001), the composer Howard Goodall describes an occasion when, having a commission to write a mass to an urgent deadline, he found himself unable to proceed. And then suddenly, one night, the music seemed to emerge from a dream-world, some imaginative spring of which he was not in control. After he had recounted this story in a lecture, a member of the audience got up and said, 'I need no further proof of the existence of God'. Goodall reflected on this answer:

'I know that Christianity has had a considerable if not decisive effect on the music of Western Europe – in some respects it is our music's midwife. Yet Christianity, like all the world's faiths, is an amalgam of many different things. For some, it is a philosophy for living, a template for well-integrated, compassionate human *societies*. For others, it is a story to explain and illustrate the mystery that undoubtedly surrounds us. But every time that someone tries to explain or pin down the mystery of God it seems, to me, to drift further away. Even those who have had profound spiritual experiences find it difficult to relate these to the vocabulary of the average church service. The Bible contains amazing poetry and much truth about humanity, but the stories of Moses, of the loaves and fishes, Jonah and the whale, or St Paul briefing the Corinthians don't in all honesty tell you much about the spiritual, non-conscious world. Music, because it is by and large mysterious and inexplicable itself, seems to edge back to the heart of it, to step cautiously towards the feeling of a spiritual dimension. It may be our last remaining link, in our most concrete of concrete worlds, with a way of being that we once enjoyed but have long since left behind. We cannot *prove* music has a power, we simply surrender to it because we want or need to. We *let* it move us. People with unshakeable faiths, I suspect, would describe God in such a way. When deeply religious people, though, replace a sense of mystery with a sense of *certainty* they are marching back down a man-made road of proof and empiricism. Music is not certain or solid or real. It operates solely through our heads and our bodies. It contains doubt and uncertainty, it exudes sadness and longing. It radiates into us, or floats past us. It is not really under our control, it has a chemistry all its own that composers tinker and dabble with. Composers are merely carriers, drawing water from a gigantic well to some parched and needy tribe, stranded far away from their natural homeland. When they first taste the water, the tribespeople think they can see their old country, hear their lost children playing, feel the old breeze on their faces. After that first heavenly sip they feel sure they will be able to find their way back home. But soon the cup is empty and they are standing once again in their new, empty, surroundings, thirsting for more.'

There is more than an accidental link between music and religion. For some people at least, they are together answers to the longing for a return to paradise lost.

Howard Goodall is right to say that this is not the domain of certainty or articulated propositions that can be proved to be true. It is rather the place where we may, through our sensory experience, glimpse something else, something that all human beings aspire to, something that is secure, beyond time and change. Within this place we can contemplate the birth and death of individuals against a backdrop of something permanent, God or Nature, *deus sive natura* as the atheist philosopher Spinoza put it. For some people, religious stories, God's promises, the sacred law dictating how we should live our lives, the hope of salvation or of resurrection, are a crucial part of the vision. They afford the moral dimension of the security for which they long. For others, any religion is too prescriptive, too precise, simply too rule-governed or bossy to satisfy their free Romantic spirit.

They may believe that the religious vision embraces moral aspirations as well as aesthetic glimpses; but as soon as moral certainties are claimed, then dissension and authoritarianism enter, and the vision is lost.

Yet it seems to me that there is no possible argument for holding that religion is outdated, or that it can be wholly replaced in society by science or any other imaginative exercise. The only thing is, it is no longer compulsory. Just as there are some people who throughout their lives have no literary sensibility, or are tone-deaf or indifferent to the visual arts, so it is with religion. The long story of Judaism, and Christianity emerging out of it, has nothing to say to them. The symbolism and the metaphors for them are dead. It is only the belief that religion is the sole source of morality that made people think that everyone *ought* or *had* to profess a faith. Of course, as I have already allowed, there are many religious people for whom their faith is the source of their morality, and their inspiration to do good rather than harm. And there are many others, who, though not especially interested in the doctrines of the Church, yet assume that the point of religion for those who retain their belief is to make them better people. But there are many others who are equally morally inspired by the thought of the needs and sufferings of humanity, the condition of this world and their involvement in it, without reference to another. So the answer to the question I posed at the beginning of this chapter – is religion as necessary to society as morality and the law are necessary? – is No. Religion is optional. Morality and the law are not.

However, that is by no means the end of the matter. Religion may not be necessary, but it may be good. First, not only children but all of us learn through stories, and the stories of the New Testament may teach morality as nothing else can, in vivid and memorable form. There is the story, as far as we know it, of the life and death of Jesus, resolutely determined to replace the old law by a new law of love, defying authority and convention, regardless even of crucifixion, pointing the way to an innovative morality infinitely wider than that of Judaism, and, ideally, including everyone, not just the chosen people. Then there are the parables, deliberately used to teach, and still effective today; proper stories with a point, a moral, and often revealing new meanings as they are repeated. Though Christianity may not be necessary to morality, indeed may often stand in its way through undue dogmatism, yet it can be a rich source of morality all the same.

Second, there are times in individual lives and the lives of society when events occur that are profoundly emotionally and morally significant. In such moments we turn, or many of us do, to long-established and traditional rituals, ceremonies that are a part of our culture. The death of someone we have loved, for example, may seem to require that we mark it, not just by private grief but by a symbolic act, an event in which we and others can take part. We *do* something, with words and music, that has to be done. There is no civilisation that does not have some such conventions. The occasions when we need such ceremonies may be much more public, like the days of prayer held at some stages in the Second World War, or services of thanksgiving that a war is over. At such times, huge congregations assemble in churches and cathedrals all over the country, briefly to share the same thoughts; and this in itself can be an inspiration, a deeply moving phenomenon. Whatever the individual beliefs or disbeliefs of people who take part in such ceremonies, such ceremonies are a bond, and an expression of shared emotion that society would be greatly worse without. Moreover, some people at least, though they do not believe in a personal God watching over them, nevertheless sometimes need to behave *as if* there were such a being; their emotion may be a sense of a generalised gratitude, a generalised remorse, a generalised sense of pity and sorrow for the sufferings of others. For many such people, of whom I am one, the rituals and the metaphorical language of religion, their traditional religion, is the most accessible and the most fitting expression.

Third, the more we think of Christianity as an Aesthetic Idea, the more we must reflect on what our particular society (and of course many others) owes to Christianity, in respect of language, architecture and music. As I have suggested already (and as Ruth Rendell bemoaned), we have almost lost the shared and beautiful language of Christianity already. But we have not lost our cathedrals and churches, or our tradition of choral music. English cathedral music is incomparably great, and this is not due simply to the music itself but to the professionalism and extraordinary education and training of the choirs, by which small boys learn the disciplines and demands of the most complex music, to their great benefit, and above all to ours. The Church of England has its own duties, and high among them is the duty to ensure the maintenance of our churches, and the handing down of our musical and liturgical tradition. To lose these things, though it might not be the end of society, would be its incomparable spiritual loss.

It is argued by the militant atheists that religion has done enormous harm, by its bigotry and moral imperialism. I would agree that, without going back to the Crusades or the Inquisition, one can lay immense suffering at the door of the Roman Catholic Church, with its insistence on the evil of contraception, and the consequences for the control of AIDS. And no one could deny the atrocities committed in the name of the fundamentalist branches of Islam. But in these and similar cases, it is not religion itself that is to blame, but the belief that religion can provide unassailable moral truth, and, above all, that it has the authority to enforce what its morality dictates. This is what does the damage, and has always done so. The Chief Rabbi, Jonathan Sacks, in the course of discussion after a lecture he had delivered in 2009, observed that the advantage of being a Jew was that, over 2,000 years, you had learned 'to sing in a minor key' in a society which you did not dominate (see Libby Purvis in *The Times*, 9 November 2009). The early Christians, until the conversion of the Emperor Constantine, had the same experience. But in no sphere is it more true that power corrupts; and Islam has been a theocracy from the start. What a democratic country must guard against with constant vigilance is any assumption of political authority by religious people on the sole ground that they are religious, and therefore have access to moral and political truth. Christianity has a place in our society, as do other religions, but it is not this place.

I suspect that it is only those who hold that all truth must be literal truth who argue that, if you cannot subscribe to the literal truth of religious teaching, you must throw it out, and all religion with it. Do so, and it would probably come back, as to some extent it has in Moscow and St Petersburg. The life of a society could no doubt go on without religion, though it would be aesthetically and spiritually the poorer if it attempted to do so. Nevertheless, we must insist that, for individuals and societies alike, religion is optional. There is no obligation to believe. And this is because the narratives and the rituals of religion were created by the human imagination to manifest the essential truth that human beings need morality to survive. We can cleanse our literature of all mention of Moses, or Jesus or any prophet of God, if we think we have outgrown stories. But what we cannot afford to do is to throw out the meaning and the purpose of the Ten Commandments, or the Christian reinterpretation of them. We cannot throw out morality, along with the stories that were invented to encapsulate it. Morality is the recognition of our common humanity, and from morality flows the law and the very possibility of civil society.

other religious organisations were exempt from anti-discrimination law in their appointment of strictly religious officials such as priests or bishops, there was no exemption from prosecution if they discriminated against non-believers or believers in a different religion or against women or homosexuals when examining applications for secular positions such as those of accountants, youth workers, vergers or gardeners. The current law took for granted that such discrimination would be unlawful, but did not make it explicit, and the churches had been acting on the assumption that exemption from the anti-discrimination law was their right, whatever sort of appointments they made. This amendment, hustled through the House of Commons, was heavily defeated in the House of Lords, on the grounds that it was an assault on freedom of worship, a long-established and hard-won constitutional right. Now, at last, people of strong religious faith declared their hand, not relying on secular moral arguments, as they had so often done in the past when matters of life and death were debated. Instead they spoke for religion itself, claiming for it a position outside the secular law which requires equal treatment for all citizens. In debating this case, they were not forced to make embarrassing avowals of personal faith, but could join forces to defend what they held to be the proper position of religion, under the guise of defending freedom of worship. Outside Parliament some people, including the influential columnist Simon Jenkins, agreed. Writing in the *Guardian*, he argued that people should be allowed not merely to believe whatever they wanted, but to live by their beliefs. If they objected to homosexuals on religious grounds, they should be free to reject them as candidates for appointment, not merely as priests but as pension managers. More generally, he argued against the encroachment of the state into people's freedom, and saw this clause as a last straw. I cannot think that he was right.

The House of Commons had had little time to debate the issue. What was horrible about the debate in the House of Lords was that, under the guise of defending religious freedom, many people simply expressed their deep prejudice against women as bishops or homosexuals as priests. Those who spoke in favour of the Government's proposal rightly saw the Pope's intervention as just such another expression of prejudice, made more intolerable by the fact that English law was none of his business. The religious view prevailed, and rather than lose the whole Bill (since time was running short before the end of the Parliament) the Government gave in, and dropped the contentious clause. It was not a good day for equality; but it could be argued that this was not a matter of enormous importance. Among all jobs, jobs working for religious bodies do not number very high. It was a worse, much worse, day for the supremacy of law over religion.

The danger of religion, any religion, lies in its claim to absolute immutable moral knowledge which, if justified, would indeed give its adherents a special place in instructing others how to behave, perhaps even a right to do so. But the laws of God, or Natural Laws to which the Pope claims privileged access, are in fact moral principles which may change over time, may be reinterpreted or given new sense by people of imaginative genius or revolutionary spirit, and in some cases may be flatly rejected. To regard such principles as the unique possession of people who hold certain metaphysical beliefs is to demean the status in society of people who do not hold such beliefs. And if there are numbers of people in society, perhaps a majority, who do not believe in a supernatural God with an interest in the behaviour of human beings, what is the meaning of the demand that religion return to politics? To believe that there exists such a personal God, made in Man's image, is not something you can resolve to do or try to do, as you can resolve or try to be nicer to your neighbour. Nor can atheists suddenly decide after all to believe in God, and become religious, as they might decide to begin going to films or listening to a certain kind of music. But if this is impossible, then the only meaning

Index

Index

Index